The YOGA of WEALTH

The YOGA of WEALTH

5 SPIRITUAL KEYS TO CREATING UNLIMITED WEALTH

Vikas Malkani

TIMES EDITIONS

Reprinted 2004

Editor: Katharine Brown-Carpenter
Designer: Geoslyn Lim

Published by Times Editions—Marshall Cavendish
An imprint of Marshall Cavendish International (Asia) Private Limited
A member of Times Publishing Limited
Times Centre, 1 New Industrial Road, Singapore 536196
Tel: (65) 6213 9288 Fax: (65) 6285 4871
E-mail: te@sg.marshallcavendish.com
Online Bookstore: http://www.timesone.com.sg/te

Malaysian Office:
Federal Publications Sdn Berhad (General & Reference Publishing) (3024-D)
Times Subang
Lot 46, Persiaran Teknologi Subang
Subang Hi-Tech Industrial Park
Batu Tiga, 40000 Shah Alam
Selangor Darul Ehsan, Malaysia
Tel: (603) 5635 2191 Fax: (603) 5635 2706
E-mail: cchong@tpl.com.my

National Library Board (Singapore) Cataloguing in Publication Data
Malkani, Vikas.
The yoga of wealth : 5 spiritual keys to creating unlimited wealth / by Vikas Malkani. — Singapore : Times Editions, c2004.
p. cm.
ISBN: 981-232-818-1

1. Happiness. 2. Self-actualization (Psychology) I. Title.

BF575.H27
158 — dc21 SLS2004007907

Printed and bound in Singapore

One who pursues materialism alone goes into great darkness,
one who pursues spirituality alone goes into even greater darkness.
Yet one who pursues materialism and spirituality side by side
(like the two wings of a bird) is happy in this world
and the next.

ISOPANISHAD

DEDICATION

To G—the Master of all Abundance!

He is the bestower of life,

He is the bestower of love,

He is the bestower of wealth.

ACKNOWLEDGEMENTS

To my Guru, Swami Rama,
whose grace brought all knowledge to me.

My gratitude to Anil Bhatnagar, my dear friend and a best-selling author himself, who helped make my ideas easier for readers to follow, especially in the action points.

My sincere thanks also to my Publishers at Marshall Cavendish for believing in me and my vision and enabling this knowledge to reach the world through this book.

And finally to my editor Katharine...you have polished the diamond and revealed its beauty. A soulful thank you.

TABLE OF CONTENTS

PREFACE

Union (yoga) must originate from separation. Just as separation originates from Union.

The creation of unlimited wealth must originate from destruction. The destruction of limited ideas, mindsets and thought patterns.

Only when you break down what is impossible does what is possible become possible. Only when you break down the idea of what can or cannot be achieved will infinite opportunities be created.

Let me therefore begin by shattering a much-believed and deeply ingrained myth. The myth that the following three 'Ss' cannot harmonise:

* Success
* Sensuality
* Spirituality

There is a spiritual way to both success and sensuality. The way is not difficult. On the contrary, it is a beautiful path that gratifies all tastes. It caresses your emotions, it lingers in your mind and it sharpens your senses.

Come, let me share a secret with you. A secret based on the hidden spiritual science of creating unlimited success. Here, thoughts blossom and, from the intangible, become real. Here, the roots of awareness are firmly entrenched by your beliefs and conscious choices are made. Here, you will surrender to the experience of being. You will become detached. You will enjoy the fruits of ecstasy.

This Union brings together the physical (senses), the emotional (feelings), the mental (thoughts) and the spiritual (awareness), thus manifesting perfect harmony between you and your outer abundance.

Walk firmly for the earth beneath your feet is not an illusion. It is as real as the world you live in: vibrant and demanding but also giving, nurturing and enriching. This world allows you to make of it what you will, to live your dreams, to create your reality.

Embrace your destiny, your destiny to be wealthy. Unite with Abundance.

I offer you *The Yoga of Wealth*.

INTRODUCTION

My Master used to frequently remind me: Living with true awareness means to live like the lotus does. The beautiful lotus flower grows out of and derives its nourishment from muddy water while existing pure and unblemished above it.

The lesson here is that neither our inner nor outer world must be neglected. In fact, we must learn to master our outer abundance as much as our inner awareness if we are to exist in true fulfilment and harmony.

Born into, brought up and trained in a business family of high repute, I lived life in the pursuit of wealth until, at the age of 29, my own self-awakening happened. Destiny then led me to the role of being a teacher who spread the message of spiritual empowerment to the world.

A few years ago, with the belief that the creation of anything originates within our inner being, I began the task of charting the map of unlimited abundance, both within and without, in humility, emptiness and earnestness.

I studied the many books and materials available, those written by the metaphysical masters and those written by contemporary wealth creators. I carefully sifted through the scriptures of different faiths and beliefs. I spoke to many leaders at the top of their professions, those at the summit of personal achievement.

With the research done, I stilled myself, meditated and prayed, waiting for inspiration from within. And when it came, I wrote.

I collated the knowledge that came forth in the form of interactive teaching, calling it The Yoga of Wealth. Over the last five years, this teaching has transformed the lives of thousands of people worldwide who have had the faith and courage to be open and practise the concepts taught within.

This book offers you the complete map to unite yourself with unlimited abundance—an abundance without boundaries, except the ones you create for yourself.

It has already made thousands wealthy and successful. Make yourself the next one to unite...

Believe me, it is your destiny.

ABOUT THE AUTHOR

An internationally renowned spiritual teacher and an expert on motivation, leadership and human relationships, Vikas Malkani has been a guest on numerous TV and radio shows and lectured at seminars worldwide.

A best-selling author and the founder of Soulcentre, Malkani is a regular contributor to numerous publications. From the cover story of *India Today* to the front page of the *Times of India*, his work has been profiled in, among others, the *Hindustan Times*, *The Asian Age*, *Outlook*, *First City*, *Life Positive*, *Around Town*, *Training and Management*, *India Abroad* and *Financial Express*.

A gifted orator, he speaks straight from the heart on how to achieve success and create happier relationships. His is a direct, simple, one-on-one approach that invariably leaves his audience fulfilled.

Malkani was presented the MC Bhandari Memorial Award in 1999, an award that is a tribute to someone who has excelled in spreading awareness and carrying out life-transforming work in the field of human consciousness. He has also been honoured with the Bhaskar

Award for promoting ancient Indian wisdom.

And that is what Malkani does best. He harmonises the teachings of the spiritual texts of the East and West, blending them to bring together the body, mind and soul.

Regarding all this, Malkani says, "I believe that my self-belief is the most important ingredient of my success in life. I believe that I believe in myself more when I believe in God. I believe that I am limited only by the limitations of my own vision. I believe that my success, then, is up to me...and God with me."

vm@vikasmalkani.com
www.vikasmalkani.com

ABOUT SOULCENTRE

Soulcentre conducts transformational programs worldwide for corporations, adults and children on spirituality, self-awareness, success, leadership and relationships based on spiritual wisdom.

For a complete list of products or information on Soulcentre programs conducted in your city/country, go to:

www.soulcentre.org
or
www.vikasmalkani.com

Nothing Changes Until You Do

CHAPTER ONE

THE AROMA OF AWARENESS—TO BE

You see things; and you say, "Why?"
But I dream things that never were; and I say, "Why not?"
~ George Bernard Shaw

Have you ever wondered why some of us have money while others have peace of mind? Is it not possible to have both? Can we not be rich and spiritual at the same time? Can we not change our 'Whys?' into 'Why nots?'? Can we not link awareness to abundance and bring together the spiritual and the sensual? For a successful person is someone who can smell the path to plenty and then go about creating and following it in the smoothest and most effective way.

Great masters draw our attention to the fact that all the wealth you will ever need already exists somewhere. It only needs to be attracted into your life. But how do you do that? By becoming a magnet that draws it to you. And how do you make yourself a magnet of abundance? By being detached from the outcome of your actions and by being aware of the timeless principles of nature, rubbing them on your belief system until you begin to respond to every small and big life situation using these very principles.

Once, my Master initiated a plan for an enormous hospital to be built in the mountains, obviously at tremendous financial cost. Hearing the figures involved in its construction, which ran into millions of dollars, I began to have doubts and asked him, "This plan and project is well and good. It will help thousands and ease their pain and suffering. Your vision is beautiful, Master, but from where will all this money come?" Amazed at my question, he looked at me and simply replied, "From wherever it is now."

That is proper awareness—that there is only One. Nothing else exists. And that One dwells inside us, outside us and all around us. In fact, we literally swim in an ocean of the One. Now, if the universe is only One, seamless and without limits, then where does creation begin? Obviously from within. With the arising of desire.

> It is the inner being of a person that is the all-important root so we should all live in awareness of our inner self.

It is from within that we develop our potential world as that is the secret of manifestation. A successful person can be defined as someone who can simply look at success as a process, a natural, struggle-free, spontaneous extension of his desire, for then he is able to complete the circle of his being, from his innermost awareness to his outermost material abundance. He bridges the two extremes, the two poles.

We utilise this science to create whatever we want because the universe exists only to fulfil our dreams and desires. It has no other purpose. If it is unlimited abundance we want, we will get it. We just have to be aware of the field of consciousness that is in existence, and ourselves in it.

If wealth and abundance attract you, then they are already a part of your inner awareness. You need only accept it.

There is a spiritual, natural way to succeed. It leads to the union between you and unlimited wealth, and it takes life from within you.

It begins with a root. This root is awareness. If you come from a root of lacking, you will proceed in this manner. There will always be emptiness within you. But if your root is one of abundant awareness, you can nurture and nourish it and create the fruit of plenty. You will get a whiff of success.

The root is the essence. It springs from the very awareness of being. Therefore, the root is of great importance. It has always existed and is the reason for the creation of the fruit.

So begin with an awareness of abundance. Do not think you are deprived of anything. Remember that the universe is intelligent. It listens to you and it will give you whatever you desire, provided you ask for it and are willing to give for it.

To fulfil is the inherent nature of the universe. Do not hesitate, ever. Reach beyond the stars but remember to start with a firm belief that you *will* get what you desire.

As the great teacher Paramahansa Yogananda put it, simply and succinctly, "The whole universe has been created by the Divine Will and when you are attuned to it, whatever you want is accomplished just by mere willing. I dare not even wish anymore, for I know whatever is in mind will come to me."

So you want to be rich, successful and spiritual? Yet, for thousands of years, heightened awareness has somehow become de-linked from material success. So now it is believed that whoever is spiritual cannot be successful. But that's just not true.

If a person is aware or walks the inner journey, he can also be extremely successful in the outside world. This is because the spiritual state of being is essentially of the inner self. Here is where all your thoughts take root, your consciousness develops, your attitude manifests itself and you become the person that you are.

It really does not matter what you do for a living, who your friends are or what your bank balance is. The inner being of a person is what is important as that is what leads to the creation of a materially successful human being. Unfortunately, most of us do not know this secret yet. But just because we do not know it does not imply that it is not the truth.

All the great masters of this world, regardless of their religion or culture, knew about this secret science of uniting with wealth. We call it a science, as opposed to an art, because it has guaranteed and consistent results. You perform the action and the relevant result occurs. That is why it is a science. Fire will burn irrespective of the person whose finger is placed in the flames.

The de-linking of spirituality and abundance is actually something very detrimental to the concept of spirituality, which encourages wholeness and totality. It has created a misguided impression in people's minds. It makes us believe that if we want to walk the path to awareness, we have to give up all the pleasures, wealth and abundance of this world. Thus, at the beginning of our search for abundance, we start with the process of exclusion.

In reality, however, one of the basic commandments that we follow in our spiritual quest is the belief that God creates everything around us for us to enjoy. We are to enjoy it, take care of it and leave it behind. The de-linking of spirituality and abundance has created limiting concepts and preconceived notions in our minds, which stop us from becoming successful.

To be really successful and to prove that you can be both rich and spiritual, let's start with the first step—Awareness.

Simply put, awareness is that of The Whole. This Whole is an indivisible and seamless oneness of which we are all a part. When we become aware of it, we become aware of the soil in which the seeds of our intentions can be sown so they can grow and manifest as physical reality.

This is the real knowledge (*gyan*) that forms the root of all creation. We must channel our thoughts in the special wisdom that there is only One and that we are all part of that One.

From this Awareness, whatever you wish for is also the wish of the universe. From this Awareness, the universe will always support you to realise your dreams and fulfil your desires.

In fact, research done a few years ago in Japan and the United States on spontaneous cures of life-threatening diseases such as cancer has shown that just before the cure appears, almost every patient experiences a dramatic shift in awareness. He knows that he will be healed. And he feels that the force responsible is inside him but not limited to him—that it extends beyond his personal boundaries and throughout all of nature. At that moment, such patients apparently jump to a new level of consciousness that disallows the existence of the disease itself. The diseased cells either disappear, amazingly overnight in some cases, or stabilise without causing the body any further damage. This leap in consciousness seems to be the key and it brings you to the realisation that everything, good or bad, wanted or unwanted, begins with inner awareness.

Unfortunately, entrenched somewhere deep within us is the belief that outer success and inner awareness can never mix. As Paulo Coelho, author of *The Alchemist*, observed, "Few can accept the burden of their own victory: most give up their dreams when they see that they can be realised."

Also be aware that it is not enough to merely have the right awareness and a dream. You must take on the responsibility to make it happen. So keep your vision wide, your dreams huge and watch the garden of your life blossom.

If you are constantly aware of the five secret keys that I share with you here, you can utilise them in whichever way you want. The same science should be applied if you want to succeed in your spiritual quest, in the material world, or both. Remember that whatever you start out doing, you have to begin with proper awareness if you want to be successful. As the Talmud, a collection of Jewish oral traditions, says, "We see a world not as it is, but as we are."

There are three petals on the lotus of awareness. One, that awareness is present everywhere. Two, that our own inner awareness in its original form is far superior to any awareness we can try to substitute it with from outside. Three, that awareness itself is far more important than the actual apparent reality, for without it that reality would not be created. Awareness is what makes the difference between a guided missile designed by a scientist and a pile of junk mctal.

Do you believe that the universe, and God, will support you in achieving your goals? Or do you believe the world is going to be against you? These are actually the only two thought options that you have.

As you begin any venture, the thought you should carry within is: It doesn't matter what I want to do. I can do it because the whole world supports me. God supports me and existence itself supports me. In the *Bhagavad Gita*, which is an ancient dialogue between God and man, Krishna, a personification of God, says, "I am the field and the knower of the field." What does he intend to teach us by saying this? When he states 'I am the field', he is talking about the field of consciousness and existence. And, in the same line, he adds 'and am the knower of the field', which refers to people like you and me and anybody else who understands the way creation happens and operates. What Krishna is trying to say is: I am God but I am also man. I am the field and the knower of the field, the one who works in this field, the one who lives in this field. And if Krishna says that I am God and I am man, it again confirms that we are all One.

Jesus meant the same thing when he said, "I and my Father are One." In other words, I, my creation and my existence all around me are One.

Therefore, if I say something, arising from such awareness, the universe cannot oppose it. If I want something, the universe will provide it. And, if what I desire does not exist, it will be created especially for me. You can build for yourself the dreams that you want and the universe will support you. This is a truth that you need to be aware of as you begin your journey to unlimited abundance.

As the ancient teaching of the *Yoga Vasishtha* says, "In every atom, there are worlds within worlds." Indeed, the universe is created primarily to fulfil you. But you must believe that before it can happen.

You must have faith in it before it becomes a reality. Faith in the belief that there is only One, there is no other. As it states in the Vedanta: In the beginning was the One, from the One became the many. If there is only One, and being an integral part of that One you say something or you think of something, will not that One support you and get for you what you want?

Essentially, there is nothing else apart from you. God and you are One. The universe and you are One. This is the truth you need to be aware of. This one belief is the proper awareness that you must always carry with you.

Awareness is a force that most of us ignore and undervalue. Generally we do not focus on our inner awareness or use its real power, even in the most difficult crisis situations. This may perhaps be the reason why miracle happenings are greeted with such a mixture of disbelief, awe and reverence. Yet the reality is that everyone possesses awareness and it is possible that miracles are simply extensions of normal abilities. When your body mends a broken bone, you do not consider it a miracle even though, as a healing process, it is far too complex for any medicine or technology to duplicate. It involves an incredible number of perfectly synchronised processes that medicine cannot imitate. Medically, it is miraculous.

The universe is waiting for you to decide, to choose, to command in total faith. But because you have doubts in your own mind, you create an inner struggle, resulting in a barrier in your own success. Therefore, the most important thing to have when you start out on your journey is proper awareness. Repeat to yourself: If I say something, if I want something, if I have a dream, if I have a wish, the universe wishes the same for me. It's there to fulfil my wish.

We also have to be aware of the fact, as Vedic seers have explained, that reality is different at different levels of awareness. Writers such as Neale Donald Walsch have reiterated that we create our own reality. But it all stems from our awareness—or lack of it. Think rich, spiritual thoughts of plenty and you will get just that. Think big, think success, and who will deny you anything?

As Walsch observed in *Friendship With God*, "Awareness is a state of being. You are 'being' aware. From this state of awareness, you can choose any other be-ing-ness." You can choose to be anything at all—successful, rich, whatever. Simply choose your state of being and then create it. This process is part of the secret science that assures us that abundance is, quite literally, our being, our birthright. That is the first awareness.

The second belief about awareness that you must carry within is that there is intelligence in this universe. This is not a universe of random happenings and coincidences. There is perfection in design. There is complete synchronicity. Everything here works in an ordered fashion. There is a purpose and a reason beyond what we see and what is apparent to us. In the New Testament, it is written that there is a reason and a purpose for everything under the heavens. Every incident that happens has a reason. We may or may not see it but that does not change the law that there is a reason for everything.

And not only is the universe intelligent, it also listens to you. It hears you when you say something. And you do not necessarily have to say it aloud. You can say it inwardly. The universe then does everything to fulfil you. That is how it naturally functions: it is intelligent; it does not work at random; it listens to you; it does not ignore you; and it does not turn you down. Not only does it listen to you, it also fulfils you. If you do not have this awareness when you start out, you actually sabotage your own progress, your own path to abundance.

In simpler terms, the universe is a self-fulfilling prophecy. It will give you whatever you want from it, provided you believe in it. The problem never lies outside. It always lies within.

Start out with this deeply rooted belief inside yourself:

> I am going to succeed and the
> universe is going to help me to
> do it because God is my God,
> and I am His, and the universe
> and I are One, and what I wish
> for myself is the same thing
> that the universe wishes for me.
> All is possible for me.

That's the proper awareness to start out with. Everything, in short, depends upon what you can build as reality in your inner awareness before you can see it as a reality in your external world. Whatever can be experienced on the surface of life itself—love or hatred, health or disease, lack or abundance—rises up from a deeper level within you and floats to the surface as little more than a bubble. It is all up to you. That is awareness.

The universe does not resist, oppose, fight or hamper you when you operate from such an awareness. It waits patiently to support you. A long time ago in ancient India, there was a holy man, a mendicant, who walked from village to village talking to people. Wherever he went, people gathered around and listened to him. But in one of the villages lived a young boy, who was the local bully. This bully did not like the guru, so he called his friends together and they hatched a plan to show up the guru.

The boy said, "The next time the guru comes here, I am going to make a fool out of him in front of everyone, and here is how I am going to do it. I am going to catch a small bird and put it in my hand behind my back. Once the guru has sat down, I am going to walk up to him and, in front of everyone, ask him whether the bird in my hand is alive or dead. If the guru says the bird is alive, I will squeeze it to death and thus the guru will be proved wrong. If he says the bird is dead, I shall bring it out alive, so again the guru will be proved wrong."

Well, the day arrived when the guru returned to the village. Once everyone had sat around him, the boy caught a bird, put it in his hand behind his back and walked up to the guru. The boy then said, "Master, great master, I have a question for you. I have a bird in my hand. Please tell me whether it is alive or dead." The Master paused for a minute, then replied, "My son, it is as you wish it to be."

So who won? Obviously, the Master. It is as you wish it to be. If you wish it to be alive, it is alive. And if you wish it to be dead, it is dead.

The whole universe is like that. It is as you wish it to be. At the highest level of being is the fundamental truth that the Seer and the Seen are the same consciousness. They are One and the same. There is no division. If you want to see a very dangerous world, then it is a very dangerous world. If you want to see people who are striving for happiness and awareness, then that is what is true for you. If you want to see a world that is against you and tries to hold you down, that is what you will see. And if you want to see a world that supports you in whatever you do, a universe that conspires to fulfil your dreams for you, that is what you will see. It is up to you. This is proper awareness.

Thousands of years ago, the ancient Indian *rishis* (seers) also contemplated this question of whether nature is ultimately unified. Rather than seeing space, matter and energy externally, the rishis observed that reality began internally, with conscious awareness. At any given point of time, they reasoned that a person must be in one of the three states of subjective awareness—awake, asleep or dreaming. What a person perceives in these states constitutes his reality. The ancient seers thus assumed that reality was different in each state of awareness. For example, a lion in a dreaming state is not the same once it has woken up.

From the subjective viewpoint of the rishis, the only possibility of the unified field was in a fourth state of awareness which they called *turiya*, meaning 'the fourth', or *para*, which denoted that it was beyond the three states of asleep, awake and dreaming, that transcended ordinary experience. They believed this fourth state existed everywhere all the time but was hidden, as if behind a screen, by the other three states. Some ancient scriptures declared that the fourth state had been mixed into the other three and finding it would be as difficult as separating milk from water. The rishis also said that the fourth state could be directly experienced only after the mind had overcome or risen above its normal activity. It is such an awareness that we must plunge into. Above the mind's regular capacity and normal activity.

The *Vedas*, written by the ancient rishis, give an apt analogy. Thoughts are like ocean waves, rising and falling, seeing only their own motion. They say 'I am a wave' but the greater truth, which they do not see, is 'I am the ocean'. There is no separation between the two regardless of what the wave might consider its reality. When the wave settles down, it instantly recognises that its source in the silent, infinite and unchanging ocean has always been there. The same holds true for our mind. When it is thinking, it is lost in its own activity. Only when it stops thinking does it return to its source in silence. Only then does the mind touch its source in pure awareness and the promise of infinite potential become a reality. The ancient seers taught that life is built up by our participation in it. Nothing is good or bad, painful or pleasant or hard or easy unless we make it so. Nothing is created without our participation.

The foundation for such an awareness, however, has to be strong. And total. If your foundation is not strong, let's not even move on to the next step. If you want spiritual success and abundance in this world, make sure you work on yourself first. If you cannot create success within you, it is not going to happen externally. You cannot pretend with creation. You cannot pretend with the universe. You can pretend with your friends and family, with your wife or husband and with other people in this world but you cannot pretend with God or with yourself. So if you are a failure inside, if you yourself are lying about things all the time to yourself, then success is never going to happen to you.

One of the important and necessary things on the path to success is that you accept yourself fully and totally the way you are, including your faults, mistakes, problems and phobias. Everything. You can only change when you accept yourself totally. But if you are always in denial and never see your own mistakes, how are you ever going to change them? Work on your inner self before you start to walk the path towards success. And then, when you start to walk, make sure your root is very strong. The first step of awareness is the foundation of success.

Be in this state of being as we move on to the beauty that belief brings.

Points of action:

1. Awareness means developing a habit of seeing yourself beyond your body. It means becoming aware of not only what you see but also of the one who sees. Stop yourself many times during the day and shift your focus from what you are observing to the one who is observing through you. Gradually practise being constantly and simultaneously aware of this observer in the 'background' while carrying out your daily chores.

2. Give yourself 30 minutes to write down:
   a. everything you are unhappy with.
   b. what needs to happen to make you truly happy—so happy that there is no need for you to ask for anything else. Do not doubt anything while writing. Assume that there are no limitations as to what can be possible. Ask yourself what you would do and accomplish and what kind of life you would like to lead if success was assured.

3. Success comes in proportion to your intensity of intention. Most people, however, lack burning desire. So how can you ignite and develop a burning desire? A burning desire can be cultivated by focusing on the pain of regret of having to live with your desires unfulfilled as well as on the pleasure that will accompany the

fulfilment of your dreams. The more you focus on this pain/pleasure phenomenon, the more the desire within you will intensify. And the more intense this desire becomes, the more energy or fuel you will have at your disposal to move towards achieving your goals. In the universe, everything has a so-called price tag. Pay the price and claim what is yours. If you can give all that it takes to accomplish your goals, then you will achieve them. Needless to say, you will give all that it takes to achieve your goals only if you have the necessary fuel or energy. Most people want to achieve their goals and/or dreams without paying the price—they just do not have the required energy. So pay attention to the pain/pleasure principle described above to unleash the energy required to enable you to pay the price that your goals are asking of you.

4. Take good stock of everything you should be doing on a regular basis in order to accomplish your goals. Jot these down as the essentials that will enable you to reach your goal. Ask yourself what you will do every day, every week and every month, respectively.

5. Start putting the plan into action. Every night, ask yourself what you did that day to reach your goal(s). Also ask yourself what you did that prevented you from accomplishing your goal(s) and how you can ensure that you do not make the same mistakes again. Rate yourself on a scale of one to ten depending on how much closer you are to reaching your goal (0 if no progress has been made and 10 if the goal has been achieved).

6. Describe an imaginary person you could admire the most and why.

In what ways are you similar to or different from that person? What can you do every day to become more like this person? Incorporate these activities into your daily and weekly schedules.

7. Ask yourself what your weaknesses are, what you are ashamed of and why you think you cannot accomplish your goal(s). The answers to these questions will give you three things to work on and overcome. You need to see through the following self-obstacles:
   a. The negative beliefs about yourself, others, God and the world that are keeping you from success.
   b. Guilt and other emotional blocks that you need to dissolve by understanding and forgiving yourself and others and viewing yourself as a new person free of any blocks.
   c. Lack of knowledge and negative habits that must be replaced by necessary knowledge and more positive habits.

PLAYING IT SAFE…IS RISKY

CHAPTER TWO

THE BEAUTY OF BELIEF—TO BE AND LIVE

Whether you believe you can do a thing or not, you are right.

Both ways you are right.

~ Henry Ford

When I started on my quest to experience God under the guidance of my Master, one of the first and most powerful lessons he taught me was: Believe totally that God is for you, beneficial for you. You are His, as much as He is yours.

With this belief acting as the starting point, everything else that follows on the journey takes on an entirely different flavour. It directs your awareness and attention inwards as you realise that nothing is against you—neither God nor the universe nor the people of the world—rather, it is all in your hands.

Believe in yourself, in your very being. Believe in your birthright to be a grand success and success will be yours. In fact, if we were to use another word for belief, it would be attitude. The right belief or the right attitude is what you need to achieve your goals, both material and spiritual.

Now, what is the right belief? Simply put, it is the strong conviction deep within you that builds the direction that you want to take in life. The heights you want to achieve, the lows you want to leave behind. If you want to succeed, then you will ensure that you follow the belief within you.

Henry Ford's simple statement is worth remembering. It is a mantra that you should repeat to yourself. If you believe you can do it, you can. You are right. And if you believe you cannot do it, then you cannot do it. You are still right.

Our conditioning, that is, what we have grown to believe, keeps us down as powerfully as anything else. This conditioning begins to develop from the moment we are born and become aware of ourselves. Those around us, our parents, friends and teachers, pass on to us their limited beliefs and their degree of knowledge. Accepting this as the gospel truth, we forget the fact that man was designed for excellence, not mediocrity.

Each one of us is born a miracle.
Without limits.

One day, an eagle lost an egg. As fate would have it, the tiny eagle egg was found by a hen. She took the egg home and sat on it with all the loving patience of an expectant mother. A few weeks later, the egg hatched and out stepped a tiny eagle. The bird had an eagle history, eagle genes, eagle chromosomes, eagle power and eagle potential. But because he was born into a chicken environment, he grew up thinking he was a chicken. He grew up dreaming chicken dreams, thinking chicken thoughts, playing chicken games and entertaining chicken ambitions.

In fact, he was made to feel ashamed of his eagle features. You see, even though he did not know who he really was, the other birds in the barnyard did. They met among themselves and said, "We have got to keep this bird thinking that he is a chicken. If he ever finds out that he is an eagle, he will rule over us."

As a result, the little bird became ashamed of his eagle heritage and features. The other birds made fun of his mighty eagle beak because they had little, thin, narrow, weak chicken beaks. They also teased him about his mighty eagle talons because they possessed weak, scrawny chicken feet. And he became ashamed of the rich colour of his deep, dark eagle feathers. Ironically, his greatest ambition in life was to, one day, hop, skip and jump up onto the fence post to cockle-doodle-do at daybreak like a rooster.

One day, when this confused bird was playing in the barnyard, he saw the dark contours of a mighty shadow glide across the ground. For the first time in his life, this little lost bird looked higher than the fence post, higher than the tree line and saw the remarkable sight of an adult eagle in full flight, with all its majesty, grace and power. The little lost bird was transfixed. He said to himself, "I sure wish I could be like that."

The adult eagle perceived the dilemma of the little bird and swooped down from the stratospheric heights and said, "Boy, you are not a chicken. You are an eagle! Your mighty talons were not meant to rake and scrape the ground for worms to eat but to snatch the craggy side of yonder mountain of achievement. Your eagle eyes were not meant to be limited to the narrow confines of the barnyard but to seek out the distant horizon of your unfulfilled potential. Your powerful wings were not meant to hang limply by your side but to catch the lofty winds of your immeasurable genius. You are not a chicken. You are an eagle."

Each of us can benefit from this tale. Where did we get our opinion of who we are? It is nothing but the random selection of memories of experiences and comments made by other people that we choose to remember from our past. It comes from the influence of our parents, peers and friends. Some of our ideas about ourselves are minor, such as whether we like a particular food, but others, such as what we are capable of, literally determine the quality of life we have. Everything from our job, our lover, our sense of dress to our expectations of the future is determined by our self-image.

The point I am making is that our perception of who we are is purely an opinion, an idea, and this opinion determines our behaviour. We then take our actions or the reactions of others to be the evidence that fulfils our self-image. The concept or opinion that we have of ourselves is the single most important determining factor in how well or badly we do in life, whether we will be happy or miserable. Our thoughts dictate our experiences and in no area is this more relevant than in the pursuit of our goals and dreams. If you are serious about achieving your goals, it is essential that you grasp this truth and commit yourself to taking control of how you perceive yourself and everything around you. Success lies with those who are undisturbed by appearances or circumstances. Individuals never reach heights above their habitual thought.

It is not enough to mount wings and soar into the infinite now and then. We must habitually dwell there.

If you dislike something about your circumstances, you have to make a decision today as to whether you would like to dissolve it and replace it with a more powerful condition or whether you would like to keep it because you can use it to seek sympathy and pity from others.

We strengthen whatever we consistently give our thoughts and attention to. For example, talk and think about your illness or your bad financial state and it will continue to get worse. Once you begin to feel and think about being in good health or in a sound financial state, irrespective of the reality, you will start to step out of the undesirable condition that you have been experiencing.

Negative conditions begin to melt once we make statements of truth about our potential. A sudden flash of realisation propels us into a new environment. In other words, it is of little consequence what transpired in your past. Your past is never fully responsible for your future, your present is.

So what do you believe? Do you believe that you can succeed? Do you carry the attitude within you that you deserve success? You started with the awareness: the universe is one with me, the universe listens to me, it is intelligent and it fulfils me. But how far does this awareness take you?

The problem with most of us is that, deep in our hearts, we do not believe we can really succeed. That is the simple truth. We are our own biggest problem.

Our beliefs stem from an attitude that we do not think we deserve success. We are what keeps us away from the manifestation of our dreams. We feel there are people who have done much more than us, therefore, they deserve success more. That is why they have got it. Well, it is all a matter of belief.

In fact, many a time, it is simply our own fears or the hardship we face on the way that may keep us from actually getting the life we want. One of the reasons people procrastinate and delay beginning something is because of the challenges, hassles and fear of the hardship that they imagine might emerge once they start.

Here is a piece of news that you may not want to hear. If you decide to go after a big enough goal, the hardship will surely come. It is totally illogical to hope that it won't and pointless to be shocked when it does. Trying to achieve something without the will to confront the problems is a bit like trying to go for a swim without getting wet. Problems are part of the deal. They are an essential part of the process and actually make the journey more interesting.

The amazing thing about hassle and problems is that they never seem as big the second time round. If you deal with them successfully the first time, the second time will be smoother sailing. By passing the test, you graduate to bigger problems and become more capable of dealing with them. It is like doing push ups. You struggle to do five in the first week but if you keep at it, you can do fifty a month later. Your emotions and ability to handle stress are exactly the same. Push them and they become stronger.

That is the wonderful thing about our goals and dreams. We create them but they also create us. And the accompanying challenges sculpt us into what we need to become in order to achieve these goals and dreams. Understand that our society rewards those who solve problems and overcome hardships. So don't fear your hassles and hardships when they arrive. Welcome them instead as signposts along the way that will help you to become who you need to be. If you look hard enough, you will see that they actually contain the seeds of greatness.

In life, we cannot choose the direction of the winds but we can always adjust our sails.

As for your self-belief, someone else's opinion of you does not have to become your reality. You can create your own. It is only when the roots of awareness are firmly entrenched by your belief in yourself and your capacity to succeed that you will actually make it. Then you will surrender to the experience of being. Your thoughts will blossom and, from the intangible, become real. Only then will you believe in the beauty of belief.

One day, a woman was working in her garden when a passer-by stopped and admired her garden, which was full of colourful flowers, sculpted hedges and landscaped grass. "God has certainly blessed you with an extraordinary garden," he exclaimed. To this, the lady replied, "Yes, and I am very grateful. But you should have seen this place when He had it all to Himself!"

As he went home, the passer-by realised what the lady had meant by her remark. Every garden along that road had been blessed with the same soil, meaning all the gardens had the same potential. But it was this lady who, by dint of hard work and belief in herself, had managed to nurture her garden far beyond those of her neighbours. The lady had recognised the difference between success and failure.

Good luck may help you to get to the top but it is only belief that will keep you there.

If you want to succeed, and honestly who does not, you have to carry this belief within you at all times. Work on yourself.

You have to totally believe in your own self. For instance, if you want to succeed in your spiritual *sadhana* (the practices that bring perfection in our self-transformation), if you believe that you can experience divinity, *samadhi* or *moksha* (enlightenment) or nirvana, your belief in the ability to achieve it must be total. You must be able to declare: Yes, it is going to happen to me in this lifetime. Only with that belief will you be able to give yourself totally to what you are doing. Your efforts have to match your beliefs. Together, they make a whole and propel you on to the path to success. Take full responsibility, knowing that God is behind you.

The mind is like a garden. You have to plant the seeds you want or else weeds will start to grow. Therefore, you must consciously plant the proper beliefs and thoughts. Belief is the raw material with which you build success. It is the trunk of the tree on which all else is supported. This belief comes from the hope that takes form in your imagination.

Everybody lives in hope and in the belief that, some day, their dreams will come true. Their prayers, though sincere, are actually one-dimensional for they have set goals and hope to attain them somehow. It is, however, belief that "creates the actual fact" as the philosopher William James pointed out. This is a thought that strongly comes across in the Bible as well: "According to your faith, will it be done unto you."

Think you can do it, believe in it and you have already half attained it. This is really how easy it is. This is the power that will drive you to fulfil your wishes. It is the impetus that will lead you forward.

If it is to be, it is up to me and God is with me.

It is only when hope becomes total belief that you will get what you want. So, be aware of your wants, set aside your fears, create a perfect world and then believe in it. Also believe in your capacity to build such a world.

This belief comes from what you perceive things to be. Here is a very interesting fact about life. Circumstances do not matter as much as how you perceive them. So your own perception about your circumstances is more important than what the circumstances really are. The circumstances by themselves are neutral. How you perceive them, whether in a positive or negative way, makes all the difference. It is just a different way of looking at things and believing in them.

The same circumstance can be looked at in two ways. Two salesmen from two different shoe companies in different parts of the world were sent to a town in Africa to explore the market there. The instructions they were given were precise: "We want to expand our market base. Let us know if there is a market for our products there."

Both of them got on flights to this faraway African town. They did not know each other. As soon as they reached the airport, they were hit by a culture shock. They saw people scurrying about, some of whom were wearing hardly any clothes; there was dirt on the streets; people were walking barefoot; and general poverty was all around. Both the salesmen were disheartened. They each took a cab, went to different hotels and checked in. The next morning, both of them went into town. They saw extreme squalor all around them and realised that the inhabitants did not have enough to eat.

After returning to their respective hotels, the first salesman picked up the phone and called his boss immediately. He said, "There is no market for our products. These guys don't even have money for themselves so how are they going to pay us for a pair of shoes? I am coming back on the next flight. I am absolutely fed up."

The second salesman called up his boss from his hotel room and said, "Guess what? Nobody here wears shoes. There is a totally untapped market for us."

The same set of circumstances but two different beliefs. Two totally different perspectives. One saw hope and the other saw despair.

It depends on you and how you want to look at life. It does not depend on life. No matter what happens externally to you, it depends on you and how you want to internally perceive any situation. It does not depend on life or the circumstances or incidents that are happening to you, it only depends on you.

This power of hope and belief is what we brought with us when we were born. It is within us. It is inherent in our lives. So why do you want to give it up? Remember: It is not your position that matters but your disposition.

The Buddha stated this same fact almost 2,500 years ago. He made it very simple. He said, "The whole world exists just on four levels of consciousness. The first level, the highest, is pure consciousness. And that consciousness is what perceives. So perception is created, and because of that perception, sensation is created, and because of that sensation, either an action or a reaction is created."

These are the only four levels of existence, and that is how the circle of manifestation moves. Either you act or you react after that. But everything starts as a simple thought in your mind.

Why do you always keep reacting? Why have you given up the power of initiating an action? The power that

God gave you when you were born, the power that was inherent in you at birth. Why give up the power to decide how you want to see things? Like the second salesman, do you want to see a whole market out there because nobody is wearing shoes? Or do you want to see the poverty and lack of a market?

If you can control the way you perceive things, you can actually control your own life.

In other words, if you can control your thoughts, you can change the way you perceive, which changes the way you act. This, in turn, changes your habits and behaviour, which, over a long period of time, changes your character, which ends up changing your life and destiny. The equation is simple: Change the way you think and you change your destiny.

In reality, there is abundance everywhere in God's creation. It is only that we refuse to see things in the way they were meant to be perceived. We come from a feeling of lack and insufficiency and we project them on the external world. In the bargain, we forget the ample opportunities that are there all around us. Our belief in ourselves wavers at this point and we forget to act from the source within. We merely react to circumstances.

If you stay rooted to your beliefs, you will find fulfilment in every sense of the word. You will walk in the garden of the five senses, surrounded by aroma, beauty, colours and many delights and ecstasies. It is important to remember that the whole world steps aside for the man or woman who knows where he or she is going.

We have two choices all the time. Either we can see the lack in things or we can see the abundance. There is duality everywhere; everything before you carries duality within it. Go back to the most primordial knowledge:

In the beginning was darkness swathed
in darkness;
All this was but unmanifested water.
Whatever was, that One, coming into
being,
Hidden by the Void,
Was generated by the power of heat.
In the beginning this [One] evolved,
Became desire, first seed of mind.
Wise seers, searching within their hearts,
Found the bond of Being in Non-Being.

Rig Veda

There was One and the One became two and the two became many. When the One becomes the two, you have entered a realm of duality. Everything around you has at least two sides, possibly more. But it is a world of duality in which we live, clothed in *maya* (delusion), and it is up to you to choose which one you want to see, the good or the bad, the abundance or the lack. God provides us with the ingredients for our daily bread but He wishes us to bake it.

Destiny is not a matter of chance, it is a matter of choice. It is not a thing to be waited for. It is a thing to be achieved.

Dreams are wonderful things and you should be consumed by one. Dreams inform us of who we truly are. They come from an eternal, constant part of us that is beyond our daily life. Dreams are not practical, not logical at times, and yet dreams have formed the human world in which we live. Every monument, symphony and great work of art that has been created by human hands first started as a dream. The lives of great people are the products of great dreams. Dreams are like oxygen as we all need them to be truly alive. If I wanted to see the depth of your soul, I would simply ask you to tell me what your dreams are. For they would reveal who you really are and where you want to go.

This may seem very simplistic but the enduring vision of your heart's deepest desire is more important than most people can conceive. In terms of achievement, all the knowledge in the world is useless unless you have a burning reason to apply it. Dreaming is a serious business. It can change the world. And you. It is both the foundation and the fuel of motivation, and every highly successful person we know does it.

If you want to be successful in life, you have to go for it with all the proper beliefs and attitudes.

I absolutely believe that success is ours for the asking provided we know how to get it. I believe that life is what I make of it. I believe that my circumstances, position, background and education are all secondary to the attitude and perception that I carry within myself. For me, self-belief leads to success. I find that I believe in myself more when I believe in God. I also believe in a God who is in alignment and harmony with me. And I believe that God wishes for me what I wish for myself, without limits. Or in two simple words: I believe.

It is this belief, with its exquisite splendour and its branches of hope and faith, that will take us to riches never dreamt of before. Remember: Non-belief in yourself, and in God, is not an option available to you on the path to success and abundance.

I can think of nothing more appropriate to end this chapter with than with these verses from *Believing in Yourself*:

Doubt can stop you in your tracks
It can drain away desire,
Believing, on the other hand,
Can set your world afire.
When you hold the opinion that
You can reach that special dream,
You have the edge needed to make
Achieving much easier than it may seem.
Believing in your ability
Affects the way you act,
And produces an air of confidence
Which influences how others will react.
When you believe you can achieve
And believe it with all your soul,
You possess a powerful asset
You most likely will reach your goal.

Anonymous

Points of action:

1. Make a list of all the things that you dislike about your life.

2. Examine these dislikes to see whether you hold yourself or someone or something else responsible for them. If the latter is the case, it indicates that you need to explore even deeper within yourself. It means your beliefs lack depth of inquiry. They fail to appreciate the fact that our circumstances do not stem from the acts of others but only through them. They come from only one source, i.e., our own beliefs and actions.

3. Complete the following sentence with at least four different endings: I am not as successful as others or as successful as I could be because...
   a.
   b.
   c.
   d.

4. Now imagine you are an exceedingly successful person who has been asked to advise someone with the above four beliefs. (If you find this difficult,

imagine it is your role model and not you who has been asked to mentor this person.) Imagine what the advice would be and jot it down as four new, powerful statements that could replace the negativity of the original four statements with infallible power, will and certainty.

5. Listed in the two columns on the following pages are two different beliefs about the same facets of life. Select the one that is the closest to your own belief.

The world is an unsafe, imperfect and insecure place to live in.	The world is an absolutely safe, secure and perfect place to live in. There is perfect order and justice in it. The apparent chaos and injustice is only a fragmented vision of the entire journey towards order. Fear and insecurity come when we do not believe in the ultimate perfection and justice of the universe.
The world is made up of matter and we are here to acquire, possess and exploit this matter for our comfort and happiness.	The world is not made up of things but of consciousness or an energy field that is experiencing itself.
There are only finite amounts of every resource and, therefore, the sooner and more we manage to grab and the less we give to others, the better it will be for us. We can prosper only at the cost of others and not with them.	Abundance is the very nature of the universe. Resources are unlimited because the world is made up of thoughts, and thoughts are unlimited. The expanse of the sky, the number of stars or the number of trees or apples each seed will finally become cannot be counted. And since this universe is one and interconnected, we can prosper not at the cost of others but with others only. Whatever we give to others, we actually give to ourselves as there is no one else

to receive it. There is only oneness and there is nothing outside it.

We are alone in the universe. And on this planet each one of us is an island, with our own needs and interests, which separate us from one another.

We are not alone in this universe. Separateness is an illusion. In fact, we are all invisibly connected to each other and to everything. Duality is only an illusion. Our needs and interests are complementary and not in conflict with one another.

Say whatever you want but the blunt truth is that ultimately it is what you come to acquire and possess that counts.

We cannot possess or own anything. Happiness does not come from the possessions we have but in how we feel inside and how we process our experiences. Happiness is a decision that can be made irrespective of social or economic status. Moreover, dignity is not in possessing but in deserving. The ultimate proof of possessing is being able to give. We lose all that we tend to hold on to. Only what we tend to give away remains.

Money is all-important. If you can manage to maintain a good image as well, there is nothing like it. So long as you do it smartly and without being found out.	After all the money you accumulate and the great image you manage to maintain, you still have to live with your own consciousness. If the world holds you in high esteem but your conscience does not, you will still feel uneasy and diseased. You can hide the truth from the world but not from your own self. The purpose of truth is inner peace, happiness and a light and clear conscience. It is not meant for public display. Irrespective of whether you are caught or not, what you have done follows you like a shadow. The laws of nature can never be broken; you can only break yourself against them.
There is no other world except this one and no life before or after here.	This world is only the physical manifestation of the universe we are a part of, and our stay here is only because of a temporary physical manifestation of our eternal spiritual self.
Consciousness is an accidental by-product of some chance biochemical reactions. Since life began by chance,	Consciousness can come only from consciousness. The so-called chance biochemical reactions may only

it does not have any intrinsic purpose or meaning.

accompany such a transition on the physical plane as a manifestation of the subtle invisible interaction of energy-intelligent impulses that give rise to new life. Though the universe may not have any ultimate purpose for its own existence except to experience its own oneness, the physical manifestation of life would not exist without purpose or meaning. This meaning has to be searched from within. Science cannot discover it for us.

In order to remain sane and rational, it is very important to believe in only those things that can be perceived by our senses.

When we believe only in what we get to perceive through our senses, we restrict ourselves only to what is on the surface. The Earth is not flat or stationary but this is how it appears to our eyes. A major chunk of the universe and its happenings cannot be perceived merely through our five senses. It would be a mistake to think that whatever is perceived alone exists.

It takes courage to make money. Those who lack the courage and subsequently the money really envy those who do not

Yes, there are people like that but there are also people who can see the futility of exchanging their conscience for a wad but instead of admitting that they are not smart enough, they sermonise about ethics and values.

of notes. These people prefer to trust the latent oneness beneath this whole existence than any material thing, including money, to fulfil their needs. Money comes from abundance; abundance does not come from money.

Tomorrow is uncertain so keep on accumulating. I have not been very fortunate in the past, at least don't let me ruin my future.

In the uncertainty of tomorrow lies the security of our beings. We are secure all the way—in the past, present and future. Accumulation is unnecessary as there is nothing that I need to make me happier or more complete. The need to accumulate and hoard will prevent riches from actually materialising in my life. I am grateful for all that I have achieved or earned and for all that has happened in my life, including the apparently not-so-good days as they were essential for learning necessary lessons.

Time should only be spent making or enjoying the benefits of having money. Meditation, prayer and other spiritual pursuits are a waste of time as what we regard as spiritual exists only in our mind.

Meditation, prayer and other spiritual pursuits are as necessary to me as water is to a fish. No gadget can work without first being connected to the mains. Similarly, no human can achieve his

	true state of being without being aligned to the Source, using these practices.
Intuition is the vague and accidental popping up of haphazard and disorganised thoughts. Pay heed to it at your own risk.	Intuition is the channel of guidance coming from our Source. If we open ourselves up to this channel of guidance by paying heed to it and by trusting it, we will never have to worry and we will always feel secure. Haphazard thoughts and wishful thinking can easily be discerned from intuitive thoughts with a little bit of practice.
Recognise your enemies and teach them a lesson. Remove everything that gets in your way and fight and eradicate what you do not like.	Hatred is the only enemy you have. Work for things you like instead of fighting against what you dislike. Working for peace is a spiritual experience. Fighting against violence becomes a part of what you are seeking to eradicate.
Miracles are coincidences that happen for a few of the more fortunate ones.	Miracles are real, day-to-day occurrences that happen favourably to those who are in this world but not of this world and who therefore are in harmony with the invisible principles of the universe. Miracles, however, take place

	unfavourably for those who think that they can safely ignore any such principles because the world has come into being and is governed by blind chances alone and not by any meaningful principles.
If I do not dominate others, I allow them to dominate me. I would choose to dominate before I am dominated.	The world can go on peacefully only if I enter into a situation in which everybody is a winner. A win-win solution to any problem is the only lasting solution.

How many of your current beliefs appeared in the first column? Highlight the corresponding belief in the second column, believe it to be true and repeat it to yourself many times a day. The inner emotions and actions stemming from these beliefs will help you achieve success because they are closer to timeless laws of nature.

6. Stop yourself many times during the day to check whether you are responding to life situations from an empowering belief or from a disempowering one. For example, are you acting out of truth or out of the need to please others? Are you acting out of fear of failure or out of courage to give all that it takes to succeed?

ACT TO MAKE FAILURE AN IMPOSSIBILITY

CHAPTER THREE

THE COLOURS OF CHOICE—TO DO

When you have to make a choice and don't make it, that is in itself a choice.

~ William James

So now you have Awareness and Belief. One is the real knowledge in which we exist. The other is the right attitude that we carry with us always. What comes next? Choice. The choices and decisions that you make in life. Choices, as I define them, are purely action-oriented. Unless you do something about your thoughts and beliefs, what good are they to you?

Never be fatalistic as this is one way of giving away your own inherent power and ability to create. If life has presented you with certain circumstances, it has also given you the power to choose and to act on that choice. We have created our own reality, which is the result of conscious or unconscious choices that we made earlier in our life. There are no victims in this universe.

Once you have proper awareness and are supported by the proper beliefs, all you have to do next is make a choice. It is as simple as that.

You can be aware of the right things, believe in them and have the right attitude, but if you sit back and do nothing, then obviously you cannot expect anything to happen. Only action (karma) has the capability to change you. Although it is the first step towards change, awareness by itself is not enough. It does not change you by itself. It has to be expressed in the form of an action.

Similarly, just wishing or thinking about doing something does not change you. All the knowledge in this world is not of any use to you if you do not act upon it. And that is where choice comes in.

Every moment offers you a choice, in fact countless choices. Just as this is a universe of infinite possibilities, every moment also offers you infinite potential, infinite possibility. You always have options. You have alternatives no matter what the situation. You have to pick and choose. The decision is yours to make and the consequence of this decision could make a huge difference to the rest your life.

Keep in mind that the future right at this moment is undecided, fluid and completely open. It will be decided based on your decision or indecision (nothing but another decision) in this moment.

In my own life, there were many times when I went to my Master, seeking a new technique or a new bit of revelatory knowledge. And every time I bothered him with my persistent requests, he would, in turn, repeatedly question me: Have you followed your practice? Have you pursued your discipline? These questions were his constant response to all my probing for new ways and higher teachings.

In hindsight, after my own awakening, the lesson was crystal clear. Knowledge has its own limitations after a point, and if transformation has to be manifested, it is only through the avenue of action. Everything I have talked about so far has been designed to lead you up to the moment when you are called upon to act, to take the plunge. You can have perfect awareness and strong self-belief, but if you still cannot bring yourself to act when your chance comes, you will never move forward in your life. You will just stagnate in all of your knowledge.

Whatever I have received is because of what I did, not because of what or how much I knew.

Simply put, if you do not act on what you know and what you believe, there is going to be no change in your life. Change happens, when it does, only with action. Almost every other person in this world has great ideas but people who create history are obviously not those who simply have great ideas but those who have the courage and conviction to take the initiative to translate their ideas into action.

Knowledge not put into action
is knowledge not acquired.
And knowledge acquired but not
used, or used to the contrary,
suffocates the soul.

This choice and this action start within, with the proper awareness, with the proper belief. The proper choice will lead you to abundance and riches, whenever you may choose to have them. This choice, followed by action, equips you for success, both within yourself and in the external world. It allows you to act in whichever way you want, to live life according to your terms. A choice made in this moment and then followed up by the necessary course of action is actually your present contribution to your own personal law of karma, which is operating in and controlling the manifestation of your life in all its facets. This is your key to alter your life in the present in readiness for the forthcoming and as yet unmanifested future.

The truth is that you can never win if you do not begin. A Chinese proverb reiterates this:

A journey of a thousand miles begins with a single step.

After beginning comes the action, done to the best of your ability. That means that your action must be done with persistence and perseverance through setbacks, failures and blocks. Just begin and you will then be on the path to achieving whatever you want. Do not delay. Remember that you do not have forever. It is your intention that is the guiding light here. If you follow your intention and choose to act upon it, your journey has already begun.

For the most powerful force in this world is nothing but pure and finely focused intent. A thought or a desire that is keenly focused to the exclusion of everything else becomes an intention and that is the most powerful thing in this world. It is like a seed. And a seed has unlimited potential. You plant a seed in the ground and you get a tree. But that one tree may produce a thousand seeds. And those thousand seeds, which sprouted from that original one seed, may produce another thousand trees, which may, in turn, produce another million seeds. However, all this phenomenal growth started from just one seed, this one intention. This is the immense power inherent in every pure intention that is backed by action.

Everything that you see around you was not there at one point in time. At one point in time, it just did not exist. How did it transform from non-existence to existence? Well, somebody had an intention and decided that he was going to act on it. He wanted to make it happen or, in other words, he chose to make it happen.

Without action, nothing happens. Nothing can be manifested or created. In the *Bhagavad Gita*, Krishna (God) advises Arjuna (the seeker) not to be attached to inaction. Actually, if you look at it in more depth, inaction is really not possible for us if we are alive. We cannot be inactive for even one second. Even if we sit down and do nothing, everything inside us continues to move. Even when we breathe, we are acting. That is a simple fact. So the only choice that remains open to us is whether we carry out an action consciously or unconsciously.

Krishna also offers us further guidance: act to the best of your ability. Have you ever considered what doing something to the best of your ability means? It means that you use everything you have available to you to do the action. You use your body first because that is the primary tool for action. But you also use what is inside your body, i.e., your mind and heart. Your mind (intellect) helps you to think of the right way to act. You also use your beliefs, attitude and awareness. Along with your mind, you employ the emotions and feelings that arise from your inner heart. The passion and enthusiasm that lie within you must be present in the action you perform. That is called doing a task to the best of your ability.

Be total in your action by being enthusiastic about it. Use everything that you have available to give it 110 per cent. I believe this is what is called 'going the extra mile'. You must believe that failure is not an option. A quote that aptly sums up this lesson comes from the famous

Star Wars movie *The Empire Strikes Back* where the character Yoda, a teacher, says to his reluctant student, Luke Skywalker, "Do. Or do not. There is no try."

When we begin to act firmly believing that it is impossible to fail, we bring to our own action immense energy generated from our physical, emotional and mental being. This is the gift we bestow upon ourselves when we decide mentally to stop making excuses and give our all to our lives. It is amazing how much stronger and more determined you become when you remove the option of failure from your mind. This is the emotional and mental state that we have to bring to the aspects of our lives that are deeply important to us—that we will simply give it everything we have got and will never give up until we have succeeded.

Of course there is always the chance of failure, which is nothing but a lesson about future success in disguise, but the fear of it should never put us off from starting on our journey. It is imperative that we start out positively. As I frequently say:

> There are no full stops in life,
> only commas.

Many of us fear that if we really give our all to our vision and it still does not work, we will expose ourselves to the pain of defeat and the ridicule of others. This is true as much in business as it is in love or sport. The irony is that the fear of failure causes hesitancy and that hesitancy causes our worst fears to come true. Furthermore, if we give something our all, not only do the chances of succeeding greatly increase but if, despite our best efforts, things still do not work out, it actually makes the disappointment easier to take. We will still have our precious self-respect and will be free from the nagging guilt deep down inside that we really could have done better.

Another benefit of mentally removing the option of failure and allowing yourself to give your all to the action is that the people around you will see it in you and will respect you for it. This is evident in sport all the time. A competitor may run himself into the ground but, despite loosing, is given a standing ovation by the crowd. Giving your all is an excellent way to develop your reputation.

Remember that if you do not choose to pay the cost for success, you will surely pay the price for failure. By doing nothing, failure creeps up on you. We often forget that we sow before we reap and that as we sow we reap. The actions we take in life culminate in momentum and lead us down the road that we have chosen either consciously or by accident.

Success is often defined as opportunity meeting preparation. Life itself will present you with thousands of opportunities once you start operating from the correct awareness and the proper beliefs. However, it is still up to you to be prepared enough to receive them and make them beneficial to your life. If your own preparation and readiness are missing, even the best of what life offers, and what God gives you, will pass you by.

We simply define success and failure by whether or not you have managed to create the life you want to lead. If you are constantly dissatisfied and yearning for something but not doing anything about it, then that is what we would define as failure. But if you are living the life you want to live no matter what it is, then we define that as success. It is a deeply personal thing. Another interesting thing is that if somebody endeavours to succeed at a goal but fails, when they look back on their life, they know they gave it their best shot. They did their utmost and that is all that can be asked of anyone.

It is a dangerous delusion to believe that avoiding the effort to succeed at something will have no consequences. By choosing to avoid the effort necessary to create the life we want, whatever that life may be, we inadvertently choose to fail, and there is no one to blame but ourselves. So consider the consequences of your inaction.

Another wonderful fact of life is that the smarter and harder you work, the luckier you become. There is a story about a man who was so lazy that he wanted to get rich without working for it. So he prayed to God to help him win the lottery. God appeared before him and granted him his wish. The man waited patiently for a couple of weeks but nothing happened. He prayed to God again and, this time, chided Him for not keeping His promise. To which God replied, "My son, you should have at least taken the trouble to buy a lottery ticket. Only then could I have made sure that you won the bumper prize."

You have to do your bit, and then God will do His. As the ancients taught: Do your best, and only then leave the rest to Him.

Success is a choice. It is up to you to decide which direction you want to take.

If you decide that you want to be successful, go ahead and visualise a life full of achievements that excludes failure. See yourself surrounded by wealth if that is what you want. You must see yourself happy if happiness is the state that you are seeking. You must see yourself imbibing wisdom if knowledge is what you are looking for. Peace of mind, detachment, whatever you desire, are all there for the asking. Choose what you want. It really is so elementary. You just have to believe it to be true.

Let me elaborate on one of the above desires. Just for a moment, presume that it is riches that you have chosen to have. Now how do you go about getting rich? You act accordingly. You act like a rich person. Your thoughts are those of immense grandeur. You see richness all around you. You see yourself acting from a platform of plenty. And, most important of all, you start to actually believe that there is immense abundance and richness in the universe for you. Then you follow it up by making the proper choices and taking the appropriate actions which will allow this wealth to be manifested from the universe around you, where it resides now, into your life, where you want it.

You make the appropriate and best possible choice that you can by using whatever you have in the present moment, i.e., your mind and its understanding, your past experiences, the lessons you have learnt, the advice you have been given and the powers of imagination and visualisation that exist within you. There is no other way. Listen to your gut feeling, to the voice that speaks from inside you, and then add to it a generous dose of the practical and logical ability of your intellect.

There was once a young man who wanted to be rich. He always thought big and knew that he would succeed. As a result, he worked very hard at whatever he did so that he would never encounter failure. His wealth increased. Ostensibly, he had it all: riches and all the pleasures associated with it. But then he decided he had worked hard enough. He began to enjoy the fruits of his labour to a great extent, often neglecting the work itself. Sadly, though inevitably, his wealth diminished.

The moral here is very easy to grasp. You cannot become rich and then do the illogical thing and rest easy. You have to work at whatever you want consistently and with a clear vision. Do your best and only then feel free to leave the rest to God.

So choose to do the action that you love. Become immersed in the area of work that enthralls you and brings out the passion and energy from within. A man who is passionate about his work is already far ahead of someone who is not.

Enthusiasm brings with itself untold amounts of good fortune and inspiration.

Choose also to do every task to the best of your ability by opting to walk the following steps before every action:

1. **Plan**—Plan out every action based on your enduring and constant long-term vision.
2. **Prepare**—Prepare thoroughly and to the minutest detail every task that you need to undertake.
3. **Pray**—Even after you think you have done all that you possibly can, do not think it is enough. It is now time to humbly seek the assistance of God and the universe in which you exist to hasten your journey to its fruition.
4. **Perform**—After an action has been properly planned, thoroughly prepared and prayed for, it still needs to be actually performed to the best of your ability, with full energy and enthusiasm. Everything before this stage is simply the preparation of the soil and now the seed needs to be planted.

Abundance is dependent on certain natural laws, which we need to be aware of. Primary amongst these laws is:

As you sow, so shall you reap.

This law (also called the law of karma, or action), when properly understood, brings with it the following awareness of the process of manifestation:

1. You must sow if you want to reap.
2. You will reap only if and after you sow.
3. There is a certain gestation period between the time when you sow and when you reap.
4. You will reap only that which you sow.
5. Therefore, sow the correct seeds, the ones of your choice.
6. Keep tending to and reinforcing the seeds after you sow them. Just sowing the seeds will not get you the desired result.
7. Believe in yourself and also trust the Higher Power to support you in your work.

This law also states, as we all know, that you get what you give. This brings us to the question of sharing. Give others what you have chosen for yourself. When the world around you is one of wealth and abundance and you have created it, never forget that it is not yours to enjoy alone. The colours of your choice brought you what you wanted. It is now your turn to spread the shades of your success. The more you give, the more of the same will come back to you. Put it back out into the universe, from where it came to you, in creative and productive ways. Allow more to return to you. It is like a full circle and you are very much a part of it.

The spokes of this wheel, or circle, of choice are always in motion. You choose, you act, you get, you gain and you give. Once part of this circle, you find rewards and renewal everywhere as you begin to enjoy the efforts of your actions that accompany the choices that you make. In fact, you are so enthused that you set yourself new targets and goals. You are moving all the time. You are acting. You are doing.

Do not worry if your choices are, at first, small. Small bricks make a large skyscraper and small actions, based on a constant and stable vision, create extraordinary success. Slowly, you will find that the scope of your choices widens, and you will be seeking much more. You will want wealth and riches of all kinds. And you will get them, too. Let me remind you for a moment of the path that this book is taking you on, the path of your union with wealth, which unfolds through the five senses. It is awareness first, belief second, then choice followed by the appropriate actions.

The fabric of our lives depends on choices. While choosing, remember that certain things are inseparable. Choose death, and you invariably choose life as well. Good and evil, birth and death, how can you choose one without the other? They are all interwoven. They are all stitches put there by the Supreme Master. Thus, choose carefully, choose wisely, choose with love and then act on your choice. The choice that you have the freedom to make.

Be prepared though. Not all choices will be correct and mistakes are bound to occur. But making a mistake is not a mistake in reality. It is only when you do not learn from your mistakes that you make the gravest mistake. So go ahead, make your choices and make your mistakes. And when you are back on track, you will soon find that these mistakes have helped you. You have emerged from them a stronger person and your faith is renewed.

Look also for the most effective way to act. Keep in mind that if you always do what you have always done, you will always get what you have always got. Therefore, to change the result, change the action itself.

When mistakes happen, do not take the easy way out. Quitting is not an option. Stick to your vision. Do not give up your dreams. What would have happened if Albert Einstein, Mahatma Gandhi, Helen Keller and other great souls had refused to carry on when confronted with a problem that, at first glance, seemed insurmountable? Or if they had refused to learn from their mistakes? They rose. They had the willingness to make and follow hard choices. They persevered. They were committed to their vision. And the world, along with them, is richer because of their endeavours.

They learnt to see their fears, accept them and transcend them. They understood that our fears are, in reality, the unsung heroes of our lives. They are our greatest friends and allies for our fears reveal who we think we are. Unfortunately, very few of us realise this as the sensation of fear is so unpleasant. In reality though, nothing reveals our self-imposed limitations better than our fears. The next time you want to do something but feel afraid, rather than backing off, listen to what your fear is telling you about what you believe about yourself and the situation. Rather than taking your fear as an absolute truth, look at it as an indicator of the thoughts that dictate your life.

As you become more familiar with fear, you will come to understand its nature. You will understand that as your fears contract, your life expands. Unless you confront and overcome your fears, they will keep you exactly where you are for the rest of your life. In the same way that pushing yourself physically by doing exercise makes you stronger, overcoming your fears expands the possibilities of what you are capable of and rewards you with a fuller life. This is what Ralph Waldo Emerson meant when he stated, "Do the thing and you will have the power." Run from your fears and you run from a richer life. Face them and a whole new world opens up to you.

Fear also gives you instant motivation. Whether you like it or not, fear is the greatest motivator available. It is an evolutionary tool designed to keep us alive and to keep us growing constantly if only we have the courage to accept it and go through it. One of the fastest and surest ways of conquering fear is to do just the thing that scares you. It sounds simple but it is true.

Not only will you encounter mistakes, blunders of your making or those of others, you will also have to face problems as problems exist in one form or another.

Here, I share with you what I call The Gift of Problems. This gift is based on five basic truths about any problem that you may encounter along your journey:

1. Problems exist. You will always have them. Therefore, do not deny them if they are there.
2. Problems have a limited lifespan. They will not last forever.
3. Problems contain the seed for greater benefits and growth. To see the problem and to choose to give it roots is entirely up to you.
4. Problems change you. For better or for worse, you choose.
5. Problems offer a choice as well. You can choose what your problem will do to you. You cannot choose the problem but you can choose how to react to it. For this reaction is in your control.

To be here and not anywhere else is the key to total concentration. By living in the present, we are in full contact with ourselves as well as with our environment. Our energy is not dissipated and is always available. In the present, there are no regrets. Thinking about the past and worrying about the future only dilutes our awareness of the present. Learn to focus all of your concentration on each individual moment, whether it is a voice at the end of the phone line, an image through the lens of a camera, a face looking at you or a beautiful rose garden.

> There is only now, only this moment. There is nothing else. Nothing. This is called Being Total.

The skilled master of life never tries to change things by asserting himself against them. He yields to their full force and either pushes them slightly out of his direct line or transfers their energy so that the energy can be used against them. He accepts life positively. And when events must be changed, he negotiates rather than inflicts his will on others.

Success is never achieved in the absence of problems and difficulties but despite them. It is wise to remember this. So do not be fazed by problems. Look at them as stepping stones on your road to riches. Just act to the best of your ability. This act, of course, can bring about tremendous change for only action can cause change. Nothing else can. Only action has the ability to create change. Choose to be active with the proper awareness and beliefs, and you will connect with God. And once you connect with God, just detach yourself.

Points of action:

1. Think of the problems you have faced in the last 1 year, 5 years and 10 years of your life. What action(s) did you take to resolve them?

2. Having recalled these problems, ask yourself which actions eased the problems and which actions further complicated them or gave rise to additional problems.

3. Write down your beliefs, behaviour, actions and choices that caused you most of the problems. What can you do to change them?

4. Do you believe that most people's problems are the result of certain wrong choices they made? Do you believe that bad results from bad and good from good? If yes, how often are you tempted to judge other people's bad circumstances to be due to unspiritual choices and yours a result of chance or bad luck? Next time you find yourself in an unfavourable situation, before you begin to blame it on your stars, accept it as a result of your own doing even if you cannot, at that moment, consciously see it very clearly. And then pray for inner guidance.

5. Ask yourself the following questions: Am I acting from the conditioning of the past or from the learning points that stemmed from it? Why is it that I tend to choose a wrong and self-defeating response despite knowing for sure that it is not at all in my best interests? For example, losing your temper even though you know that it is unwarranted or knowing that you are in the wrong and should ask for forgiveness but do not. In such circumstances ask yourself: Who am I obeying? Who am I trying to be loyal to? And who am I trying to protect? Watch yourself as a silent observer and dissociate yourself from the one the above questions are leading you to.

6. Whenever you hasten to say, "I am surrendering to God," ask yourself, "Am I shirking from my responsibility in the name of surrendering to God or I am doing it after doing all that I could?"

7. Do you often say, "I am accountable only to God, not to any Tom, Dick or Harry?" You do not realise that God often gives you His feedback through Tom, Dick or Harry. Moreover, when you say the above, you are, in fact, saying that if given a choice, you would not want to be responsible to anyone—because having to be accountable to God is not a choice but a compulsion.

8. If you love your family but assume that they know it without you having expressed it verbally, tell yourself that you are making a conscious choice to live a life of unexpressed love. God has given you love but you are holding it back instead of passing it on to the person(s) it was meant for. How would you feel about a postman who says, "I have done my duty of collecting letters from the postmaster. However, I am not going to deliver them. Instead I am going to keep them. Then when I die, people will find out how many letters I was carrying for each and every one of them." Wouldn't you like to tell him that a letter not delivered on time loses its purpose? Is it not the same in the case of the love that you have received from the universe around you, in different ways, through different people, at different times? It is meant to be shared and distributed. It is not to keep.

9. See each moment as a building block of your life. There is no scope for casualness, complacency or procrastination in any work of art.

Each brush stroke should itself be a masterstroke in order to create a masterpiece. A film director once said, "When I am shooting any scene, I tell myself that I am shooting the best scene of my life and I must give it my best." Our approach to our most mundane daily choices should be carried out in the same spirit. However, it is no use wasting time perfecting a scene that should either not be in the movie of your life or could have been shorter so as to leave more time for some of the more important scenes.

10. Learn to be aware of and remain in touch with inner silence. Choices that stem from an interval of inner silence are wholesome. Choices that come from the noise of a chattering mind or from the lack of silence are seeds of misery and additional problems. Develop a habit of not focusing on the world that is put together by the senses and overcome the temptation to identify yourself with it or the need to judge and react to it. Instead focus on the silence within because that is your true identity and that is what you need to respond to. Make it a habit of asking yourself: Am I in its noise or in the silence beyond it? Having asked this, tell yourself, "I am free to choose where I should be".

LEARN TO LIVE RICH, NOT DIE RICH

CHAPTER FOUR

THE DELIGHTS OF DETACHMENT —TO DE-ATTACH

He who considers himself free is free indeed, and he who considers himself bound remains bound. As one thinks, so one becomes.

~ Ashtavakra Samhita

You have taken the best possible action based on your current choices. You have the foundation of the proper beliefs and you live in an awakened state of awareness. Now, simply Let Go.

Detach yourself from whatever comes your way; surrender to the One above. This is what I call the secret spiritual science of success that is the Yoga of Wealth. You can learn about success from hundreds of sources and people, but they will not teach you what the great masters knew and practised over 5,000 years ago. They will not teach you the techniques the masters used—work hard to create whatever you want and be happy every moment of it all, whether the results are achieved or not.

In the previous chapter, I wrote about what Krishna told Arjuna:

> Do your action to the best
> of your ability.

Now let us move higher as Krishna also adds:

> But without attachment
> to the fruit thereof.

To do the action to the best of your ability is the choice that you make. Put everything that you have into what you are doing. Give yourself totally to it, empty yourself in its very doing, surrender yourself. You are then so focused that nothing else obstructs you.

There is a small incident in the *Mahabharata*, the great epic of ancient India, that serves as a learning story for us all. It tells of a wise archery teacher named Drona who taught the warrior arts to the Pandava and Kaurava princes. After he had taught the five Pandava brothers the basics of archery, he decided to test them to see which of his students was the most qualified for higher learning. He gathered them together and said, "I want to see who has learnt the most. See that deer ahead of you? It's a dummy that I made for you to practise on. I want you to shoot the deer from where you are standing but shoot it only in the eye."

Yudhishtira, the eldest of the brothers, was the first to try. He strung an arrow but before he could fire, Drona asked him, "Well, what do you see?"

To this, Yudhishtira replied, "Master, I see the deer and I am to shoot the eye. The forest is behind the deer."

After hearing this, Drona told him not to shoot.

The second brother then came forward. After he had strung an arrow, Drona asked him the same question. To which the boy replied, "Master, I see the front part of the deer. I see the head and the eye is in the head. I have got to shoot the eye."

Drona then asked, "What's around the deer?"

He answered, "Well, there are trees and there is grass."

Drona also told him not to shoot. And so it went on.

The last person to be tested was Arjuna. He cocked his arrow and was ready to shoot when Drona asked him what he saw.

Arjuna replied, "I see the eye."

"Do you see the deer?"

"What deer?"

Then Drona asked, "Do you see what's around the deer?"

Arjuna replied, "What deer? I see only the eye. That's what I'm going to hit. I don't have to see the deer. I don't have to see what's around the deer. I just have to see the eye because that's what I'm going to hit."

Arjuna was detached to everything but his chosen intention. He did not see anything except his target. That is the kind of focus that is necessary if you want to act to the best of your ability. And do remember that focusing on one and one target alone automatically signifies detachment from everything else. This is what is called 'being total in the moment'.

That is what Krishna wanted from Arjuna. And that is what God wants from all of us as it is what we need to achieve success and abundance on different planes.

God is with us constantly. It is us who are away from Him. If you have the eyes to see and the correct kind of awareness and belief, you will see God every time you turn around. He is behind you right now. And He is saying to you, "Well, why don't you move forward? I am with you. I am always with you. I am behind you. I am supporting you in whatever you are doing."

The problem is that we just don't believe Him. How many of us walk through life believing that God is walking behind us? That if we fall, He will support us? If we stop, He will nudge us forward? If we get lost, He will help us find the way? God is right behind us and is pushing us towards success. The problem is that we are afraid of success. And that is the primary reason why many of us do not achieve it or taste its strong heady flavour.

The problem lies within us, not anywhere outside, not with the world. The world does not keep us down. It is our failure to detach ourselves from our own limitations that holds us back from surrendering to God.

Or, in other words, it is our attachment to mediocrity that keeps us away from true success and extraordinary abundance. It is our attachment to many things at one time that prevents us from achieving any one thing totally at any time.

Once the best possible action is performed, it is essential to detach yourself, both from the action itself and from the fruit of that action. When you arrive at such a state, it leaves you completely open and empty to receive and accept whatever follows.

True surrender is to expect nothing.
And, at the same time, to be open
to everything.

Rather than expect a specific result, what you can do instead is to remain open and pray. There is power in prayer, in faith.

There was once a little boy who was trying to move a big boulder in his parents' backyard. He tried everything possible, using all his strength, but the boulder would not budge. Noticing that he looked dejected, his father, who was watching him, asked him if he had tried all the possible ways to move the boulder.

The son replied, "Yes, father. Of course I've tried everything. It just won't move."

The father then pointed out, "No, you have not. For example, you have not asked me to help you. Together I'm sure we could move it easily."

God is our Father, the creator of everything, omnipotent, omnipresent and omniscient. Then why do we hesitate to turn to Him for help? Here's a secret—make God a partner in all your endeavours. Keep Him by your side. Let Him dominate your actions. Seek His support rather than resist Him in every step of your journey.

Like Arjuna, we should be totally focused on our action and the goal it is leading up to and detach ourselves from everything else. The rewards will follow as we achieve whatever it is that we were looking for. That is the extremely important and mostly overlooked spiritual dimension of success. It keeps you happy and relaxed throughout your journey to unite with wealth even though you continue to work extremely hard and give yourself totally to your work. Both go together: first the total action and then the total giving up of it. It is almost contradictory—enjoy your rewards but also be detached from them.

My Master was the head of a large network of people, organisations and books, the cumulative value of which ran into millions of dollars. At the same time, he was always initiating new projects, even before the earlier ones had been completed. It seemed he moved with the force of a whirlwind for he single-handedly performed the work of ten men.

However, during all of this activity, I always saw him completely detached from it all, immediately after the action required was finished. He was fully present during the effort, following which he became completely free and relaxed. He was totally centred within while performing his action to the best of his ability in the external world. He totally lived by the philosophy 'Let go, and let God' but only after he had performed the highest possible action.

Let me ask you a simple question. You take two good seeds and plant them in well-prepared soil. You plant them with the correct awareness and you believe that they will grow. You have operated with the proper beliefs. You have even planted the seeds properly, at the right time, and were totally committed to your action. You did your very best. But even after all that, can you guarantee that both of the seeds will sprout? The answer is no. Maybe one will while the other will not. Maybe both will or perhaps neither will.

Now you may wonder why this is so. The reality is that final success depends on a lot more than just what you do right now. It depends on a million other factors falling into place at the right time. So don't be attached to the fruit of your action. There is no way that you can guarantee where the action will take you. Do the action to the best of your ability, give it all that you can and then detach yourself from it, thereby allowing it to mature and manifest with the help of the universe and God. Attachment after this point will only obstruct the process of fruition.

Detachment is something you do effortlessly. You cannot struggle with it. It happens naturally because it is like love. You cannot fall in love by making an effort. It is also like enlightenment. These things happen by themselves; they cannot be forced.

You arrive at detachment when you have done your best and let go of the action rather than hold on to it. You let it go out into the universe. And when you do, you allow the universe and God to take over and complete the process of bringing the result of your effort and action back to you.

Our actions never really trouble us. It is the constant thinking about them and the subsequent worrying about endless possibilities that trouble us. If you have a big task ahead of you, actually doing the task will never bother you. However, thinking about it all the time will. This happened to me recently. I was on a long-distance flight, the duration of which was bothering me. I hate sitting for 9 hours at a stretch in one place. Worrying about it was obviously not helping, so I told myself to stop worrying and allow myself to let go. And when I did, I realised how easy it was.

In reality, holding on to something is actually far more difficult than letting it go. When holding on, you are never relaxed. You struggle because you don't want to let go. You keep on grasping, an action that requires strength. However, if I were to tell you to relax, it would happen automatically. This is how 'let go' happens. Just completely relax after you have done your best possible action.

Relaxation is the most important part of letting go.

As long as you are tense about something, you simply cannot let go. So don't hold on to things so tightly. Since these are the very same things that disturb you, why don't you just let them go? The most interesting fact is that nobody is telling you to hold on. You continue to do it blindly, with your eyes and awareness closed, even though it constantly troubles you and causes misery. Nobody forces you to hold on. The simplest thing to do is to let go.

Be careful though as there is a trap here. The action must be done to the best of your ability, i.e., 110 per cent, before let go happens. Otherwise, you will not be able to truly let go. You cannot do something half-heartedly and then say, "Well, I'll let go of it and now it is up to God." This is the crucial secret and the stage at which most people fail.

How do you know when you have reached the stage at which you know you cannot do anything else? The answer is simple. As long as you feel you can do better or more, keep doing it. As long as you feel there is something you can still improve upon or have not thought about or done, keep doing it. And when you reach the point at which you feel you have done the best for that action, that you can't do anything else, let go. Simply detach. It is no longer in your hands.

Ponder the wisdom in this poem titled *Let Go and Let God*.

As children bring their broken toys
with tears for us to mend,
I brought my broken dreams to God
because He was my friend.
But then, instead of leaving Him
in peace to work alone,
I hung around and tried to help
with ways that were my own.
At last I snatched them back and cried,
"How can you be so slow?"
"My child," He said,
"What could I do?
You never did let go."

Lauretta P. Burns

You have planted those two good seeds in the soil. Now, what do you do? You cannot dig them up every other day to find out if they are growing. If you do, they will never grow. No, you have to let them be. Allow them to sprout on their own, without your interference and with help from the universe.

We simply do not know what the universe has in store for us because we do not know our past actions and the awareness with which we performed them. In such a situation, it is wiser to detach and open yourself up to receiving whatever comes your way, once the best possible action has been performed.

It is often believed that success equals self-effort multiplied by grace. If we consider grace to be what God or the universe sends back to us, based on actions performed in our past, it once again brings us to the fact that we must detach ourselves from the action as well as the results of the action. Only then can we arrive at a state of openness and emptiness that enables us to receive the maximum coming to us.

There is a story about a boy, about to turn eighteen, who asked his rich and loving father for a Ferrari on his birthday. He had total belief that he would receive the gift he desired so intensely from his doting father.

When the day arrived, the boy looked forward to his father's gift with great anticipation. In front of the whole family, the father handed his son a book that was wrapped in beautiful paper. The boy, surprised, opened the gift to see a Bible instead of the keys to a Ferrari. Disgusted and disappointed with his father, he threw it away and ran out of the room in anger and shame. He did not see the tears in his father's eyes as the Bible hit the wall and the keys to the Ferrari that his dear son had wanted so desperately drop out from within its pages.

The father's message was clear: My dear son, I love you very much, and I will give you everything you want and more. However, it was the son's expectation that prevented him from enjoying the fruits that his life was presenting him with.

Get rid of all expectations and do your best.

And when you have done your best, when you have given all that you can give and you feel that you can give no more, that is the time to go into detachment. Remember: You cannot struggle with detachment; you just have to relax into it. This is the secret. Detachment happens the same way love happens, the same way enlightenment happens, the same way awakening happens.

Detachment is one of the most freeing moments ever.

You do not know when it happened or how it happened. You cannot force it to happen. But when it does, all you can say is "Thank you". All you have is gratitude at that point in time.

Another important principle of detachment is the ability to forgive. We tend to blame others when things go wrong. By doing this, we think we have covered up our own mistakes, faults and guilt. What we do not realise is that if we continue in the same manner, negative emotions will tend to rule our minds and we will become trapped in a circle of blame, guilt and judgement. And letting go will become all the more difficult.

Judge not that you be not judged.
For with what judgement you judge, you will be judged; and with the same measure you use, it will be measured back to you. (Matthew 7, 1–2)

As the wise Buddha said,

"For a truly wise man, there is no such thing as good or bad."

For such a man simply learns from everything. Such a man is completely detached from the action or the happening itself and instead keeps his awareness on the lesson within, the motivation beneath. Thus, every incident becomes simply a teacher, as all judgements of good and bad are overcome with detachment.

Once you overcome negative thoughts, you find yourself becoming more positive in your attitude and in a frame of mind that enables you to accept much more. These are qualities that a successful person requires. Forgiving others is the key to being total and doing your action fully, which eventually results in success.

When you forgive, forget and detach yourself, you are in bliss. You are now able to turn your consciousness to better thoughts and to a much higher level.

You have done your best. You are now ready to Accept. You have begun walking the path to ecstasy.

Points of action:

1. Trust that God knows what you want but wants to give you more than what you want and that more is what is in your best interests.

2. Whenever you do not receive the anticipated results, ask yourself:
   - Have I given my best?
   - Though I want something with a burning passion, am I prepared to receive a result different from what I desire and take it as a yet undisclosed gift from God?
   - Have I listened to my inner voice? (Often the undisclosed gift is a God-sent lesson that we need to learn to ensure for ourselves an unprecedented future success.)
   - Am I taking God's delays as denials?
   - Am I asking for something that is not good for me in the long run? God displays His love best not when He is granting our wishes but when He withholds them from us. It is always easier for parents to give in than to withhold what may not be good for their child in the long run.

   Try to see and appreciate this love when things are not moving in the direction in which you anticipated.

3. Do your best, stir some love in it, ensure that there is nothing left that you were supposed to do and then, with complete trust, leave it in the hands of God. Detachment comes from the trust that once we have expressed to God our intention, God need not be told 'how'. He knows better than us what is best for us. Often those who are drowning make the job of their rescuer difficult by holding onto them too tightly, preventing them from being able to swim. When God comes to your rescue, remember to let Him do His job. Don't hold on to images or expectations of fulfilling your desires. Attachment makes it difficult for anything to flower, for any endeavour to arrive at its

fruition. Asking for the fulfilment of your intentions as per the desires, expectations and images of your small ego while asking for the best support from the universe is like asking the pilot of an airplane to follow the same route as the road lying thousands of feet below. Detachment is trusting fully in the pilot and airplane and just enjoying the flight until you arrive at your destination.

4. Instead of achievements, labels, rewards and awards, focus on making yourself more and more deserving. Glory is not in receiving but always in giving and being deserving. Dr. Modi was an Indian ophthalmologist who did innumerable eye operations every day, especially on the poor. An agency in the United States that was deeply impressed by his commitment and contribution to humanity declared him the winner of its annual international award. When informed, Dr. Modi thanked the agency for this recognition but expressed his inability to come personally to accept the award. He explained that the days he would have to take off to collect the award would deprive him of the opportunity to bring vision to hundreds of cataract patients and it would be highly irresponsible and callous on his part to do so.

Recognition and rewards are just symbols of appreciation and gratitude and whether we get them or not, God always knows who deserves and who does not. He cannot be influenced by propaganda or bribed. And to influence him, we have to have the approach of Dr. Modi. Focus on making yourself more, more and still more deserving. Recognition by society is like a withdrawal from your universal account. Any input to make yourself more deserving is like a deposit. Needless to say, prosperity comes when the deposits are endless and the withdrawals are few—just enough to manage your basic needs.

LIVE LIFE—GODSIZE!

CHAPTER FIVE

ECSTASY—TO ENJOY

Rise from dreams and loiter not.
Open your mind to truth.
Practise righteousness and
You will find eternal bliss.
~ Gautama Buddha

You are now effortlessly detached. The action has been performed, fully, in your totality. By doing so, you have become totally empty. You are now simply being. Be-ing.

In fact, by now, you have probably reached a level where you find yourself dreaming and experiencing emotions like never before. This may sound almost paradoxical but in this moment of detachment you are enjoying everything with a heightened state of awareness. Colours seem brighter; people nicer. Why, it is like paradise right here on Earth. And this has been made possible by your beliefs and your choices and, naturally, the actions that resulted from them.

Your attitude now is one of a person who is successful in body, mind and soul. Things have fallen into place. You are at peace. And in bliss, ecstasy is there for the asking. It is your state of be-ing.

Bliss, or contentment, is a state of mind, a state of being, not something that must be waited for or struggled for.

To reach this stage naturally, you ought to detach yourself from all actions. Do this only after you have completed the action, having given it more than 100 per cent. You will then arrive at a stage that is full of enjoyment, contentment and bliss—ecstasy, in other words. This happens almost automatically. It is like one step following another. When you let go, when you completely relax, and do not wait for the rewards to follow, you reach a state of contentment. You arrive at this state because you are now totally empty. And the rewards follow, the rewards that are due to you, the ones that you deserve.

To do something so totally that you become empty of yourself is a wonderful way to create the space necessary to receive. For when you do something so totally and then let go of it, a very potent emptiness is created inside of you. You arrive at enjoyment, contentment and bliss—ecstasy, in other words. This is how the Masters always worked. Krishna did everything that He had to do totally and then He forgot about it. He did not carry it with Him. When the choice was made and the appropriate action taken, He let it go, He let it be. This is also how the Buddha worked. When He wanted something done, He just said, "This will be done." And then He did whatever He had to do to follow it up, then He let it go. He just let it be and it soon manifested.

If you do something, be enthusiastic about it. Be total about it. Otherwise, don't do it. Don't waste your or other people's time. I feel that the quality of enthusiasm put into the action has not been given the importance that it deserves. What exactly does enthusiasm mean?

To be enthusiastic requires you to be passionate about whatever you do, to bathe in it, to dive deeply into it.

The word 'enthusiasm' comes from the Greek roots *en*, meaning 'within' or 'in', and *theos*, meaning 'god'. So when the Greeks first coined this word, they were trying to say that when you are enthusiastic, you are actually operating from a state of being-in-God. You are in God at that point in time when you are fully passionate about something. The *Vigyan Bhairav Tantra*, one of the most ancient scriptures of the world, talks about 112 ways to achieve enlightenment. In one of the techniques, Shiva, the ultimate yogi (master of the self), tells Parvati, his wife and a goddess in her own right, "In a moment of intense passion, dissolve and find Me."

To be truly enthusiastic is to be in a moment of intense passion. To be in God is to be enthusiastic. Be full of passion for whatever you are doing. If you are not passionate about what you are doing, true success is not for you. For someone who is more passionate than you will give more to his action and his life than you ever will.

Let's be more positive for a minute and look at it from a completely different perspective. Instead of becoming artificially energetic about what you are doing, find out what you are naturally enthusiastic about, what you are passionate about, since all of us are passionate about different things. There is a dream within all of us and, unfortunately, most of us live with a big stone placed on top of that dream. We put that stone there to suppress the dream and to stop it from coming out and talking to us. We are afraid because if the dream does talk to us, we will have to do something about it. We can't ignore it. Most of us, however, spend our lives repressing the innermost dream in our heart. We never let it out.

If you want success, you have got to be passionate, deeply passionate. Not passionate for a day or two but passionate consistently about what you are doing. All the rich people of this world, all the abundant people, all the great spiritual masters are extremely passionate about what they do.

This passion within you will bring you happiness. It raises your consciousness, makes you more aware of life and living and, best of all, it is here to stay. This reminds me of a poem titled *Gloom or Gleam* by an unknown author.

It's a cheery old world when you are
cheerful,
And a glad old world when you are glad.
But whether you play or go toiling away
It's a sad old world when you are sad.

It's a grand old world when you are great
And a mean old world when you are
small,
It's a world full of hate for the foolish
who prate
On the uselessness of it all.

It's a beautiful world to see,
Or it's dismal in every zone,
The thing it must be in its gloom or its
gleam
Depends on yourself alone.

You create your world with your thoughts, your feelings, your deeds and your attitude. The harder you work at it with awareness, the clearer you see it happening and the easier it will soon become. The fruits of your endeavours will come without fail.

The usual pattern is that we act, then immediately expect results. And then we complain if these results fall short of our expectations. Even if you do succeed, the thrill of achievement does not last. As they say, a Mercedes is enjoyable as long as you strive to get it. Once you have it, the enjoyment starts to wane and the worry increases because you have to keep the desire for it alive, forever new, forever interesting, forever attractive.

True ecstasy lies within. You create it and it remains with you.

That is the essence of a successful person. He is both spiritual and successful. It is really what he is within that makes him reach this state. He has let go of results and rewards yet believes totally and does his action passionately. He lives his life from within.

As I believe:

Life is a gift to be enjoyed with awareness.

And it is only possible to enjoy this valuable gift when we are in awareness of ecstasy.

That is the state we should all try to arrive at. We are detached, yet we have not given up our commitments and beliefs. We are aware of everything around us. A successful person is one who works hard, is passionate and works towards his vision without worrying about the circumstances around him, with peaceful inner awareness that God is with him and that 'all is right with the world'. He has left behind fear, the enemy of happiness and success. Fear of failure, of rejection, of not getting what he wants. Fear of not living up to the expectation of others.

Fear is a huge deterrent. It makes you tense and unhappy and, as a result, your mind does not function in the way that it should. You behave in a manner that seems almost alien to your normal way of functioning. Fear keeps you away from ecstasy. But if you let go of this fear and surrender to a Higher Power, to God, you suddenly find miracles all around. Things fall into place. The garden is in full bloom, with colours and emotions of your choice.

Many times in my life, I saw my Master pass through difficult and trying times, whether, for example, because of a delayed project or the work of a careless employee or student. But even as he handled many emergency situations, I never saw him truly perturbed or shaken within. Inside he was calm, peaceful and stable. In a state of enjoyment and bliss— unshaken. Whatever was happening was creating ripples only in his outer life, not in his inner state of being. During such moments, my Master's powerful words would reappear to knock on the door of my unaware mind: Let everything of this world play its dance in the world outside. Let nothing of this world do its dance inside your head.

We should be like a swan. Although her feet move at a hectic pace beneath, she glides so peacefully and gracefully across the surface of the water.

Ultimately then, a successful person is someone who has abundance both within and without. He is happy inside as he has full faith in the universe and its ability to look after him. He is the person who can live life completely. He will achieve greatness, probably without even realising it. His is the state we should all try to emulate. Nothing can upset him; a deadline gone awry, a shipment delayed. Externals are just that—externals. His seeds of happiness, the source of all this ecstasy, have been sown within. He nurtures them with his intense dedication, his passion and his belief. He does his best and takes the most effective action possible. And then what does he do? He just lets it all go. He detaches himself from the fruit.

This is what I refer to as The Law of the Seed. When a seed is to be sown, we first have to dig the ground and prepare it carefully with the right soil. Next, we have to look for a good seed to plant, which we then place into the soil. We nourish this seed with the help of water and sunshine, a process that I call Knowledge and Action. At times, the seed will sprout as we expect it to. Other times, it may not. The point here is that once we have taken all the right steps towards planting and nurturing the seed, we should let go and let God take over. We should detach ourselves from the results and then it will probably bear fruit faster than we anticipated.

If we truly follow these steps, then we must enjoy the detachment, too. The completion of the garden of the five senses is not possible without this true detachment, which must be achieved in our lifetime. This is the spiritual secret of success. The more you have, the less you should be attached to it. This is the true yoga of wealth. This will ensure that your thoughts are positive and will lead you to bliss and ecstasy.

As Sri Aurobindo, the great sage, said, "All life is yoga (union)." I believe that all life should be success itself. This begins with doing what you enjoy, preceded by a purpose and a vision for your life that begins within your inner awareness.

Your journey through *The Yoga of Wealth* is now drawing to a close. As you will have experienced, this walk has had its ups and downs, its highs and lows. At times, you may have felt like quitting; other times, you may have felt you could go on forever.

Even the way you have read this book and the level to which you have accepted its truth depend on your inner awareness. As your own inner awareness grows, so too will your perception of the knowledge given in this book be enhanced.

The way is now in your hands. You must decide the destination consciously. The journey will be made on your feet. From abundance to awareness, from the sowing of the seed to the enjoyment of the fruits of your actions, I have shown you the way that bridges inner awareness and outer success.

Striving to be rich, or wanting wealth, is not an evil thing. It is your attitude towards it that counts. You do not need to equate richness with guilt or spirituality with sacrifice. You can actually decide your own state of being, both within and without. I have spelt out what you really need to do and how you can change your attitude towards material possessions. Now you need only do it.

It is a fact that whatever you put out into the universe comes back to you. When you transmit to the universe around you that you are in a state of being in ecstasy, guess what is coming your way? Ecstasy itself and everything that is good, wholesome, abundant and fulfilling. In other words, unlimited success.

Reflect over the following: If a fire is far away, it provides you with no warmth. And if you bring it too close, it burns you. It is important to only bring it close enough so that you can benefit from its warmth. Try to adopt this attitude towards all your belongings and you will find the world is full of rewards. You will be happy, inside and out. You will have total peace of mind. And then who could be richer than you?

Creation, or existence, moves in cycles of regeneration—from creation to preservation to destruction, and then back to creation—from inner being to outer being and back to inner being. From awareness to choices to ecstasy, and then back to awareness. The circle completes itself, without beginning, without end. This process continues whether you are aware of it or not.

The secret of this union lies in seeing the process of creation clearly and entering it in an awareness of ecstasy. Then, based on the flavour of your participation in the process of creation, come the fruits.

Just as love begets love and hate begets hate, ecstasy begets ecstasy. And you unite into the very desire you manifested from your state of be-ing.

Points of action:

1. Recall a time when you felt at the peak of being fresh, energetic, fulfilled, joyful, intoxicated with the beauty of what you were seeing, contented and enthused. Knowing that it was merely an inner state, can you transpose those feelings into your body and mind in the present moment irrespective of your current external circumstances?

2. Develop a habit of ignoring external circumstances and focusing more often on the fact that you can feel ecstasy without a reason—that is what life is for. To be alive is a cause for celebration. We fail to see this when we unnecessarily link our happiness to external conditions:

I will be happy when I get my first promotion, more business, a better job…whatever. Why can't we decide and declare to ourselves, "I'll be happy to the extent of being ecstatic when I find myself breathing."

Moments not enjoyed with awareness are moments not lived.

3. When you fail to achieve a goal, instead of feeling bad, try to feel the feelings that you would have felt had you succeeded. If you do this often, you pave the way for certain success in your future attempt(s)—more so when you reform your action in the backdrop of the lessons learnt from past failure(s).

4. Develop an attitude of gratitude. Gratitude means appreciation of God's love for us exhibited in nature and in the experiences that make up our life. Gratitude necessitates conscious awareness of God's loving gifts, which we enjoy every moment. And when we develop an attitude that continually keeps us in a mental state of gratitude, it results in ecstasy and enlightenment. Practise becoming aware of your present moment and thanking everyone and everything that have made the experience possible.

AFTERWORD

When pressed for the ultimate truth, the Vedic seers uttered two words that overturn all our accepted notions of reality: *Aham Brahmasmi*. A loose translation of this phrase is 'I am the whole. I am everything, created and uncreated. I am the universe.'

To be everything, or even something beyond the confines of our physical, emotional and mental self, sounds, at times, strange. But according to the enlightened masters, it is the only truth. It is our natural state of being. And operating from this truth, there is nothing called impossible.

In one of the teaching stories told by these enlightened ancient seers, this same truth is brought forth very simply. A youth named Svetaketu was sent away from his home to study the spiritual wisdom of the Vedas. In ancient India, this meant staying with a Master and memorising long verses of sacred writings.

Svetaketu stayed with and studied under his teacher for 12 years. When he finally returned home, he was proud and full of his own learning, so his father, a truly wise man, decided to deflate him.

"Go and pick a fruit from that banyan tree," said Svetaketu's father.

"Here it is, sir."

"Split it open and tell me what you see inside."

"Many tiny seeds, sir."

"Take one of the seeds, split it open and tell me what you see inside."

"Nothing at all, sir."

Then his father said, "The subtlest essence of this fruit appears as nothing to you, my son. But, believe me, from that nothing, this mighty banyan tree has sprung. That being is the subtlest essence of everything, the supreme reality, the self of all that exists. That art Thou, Svetaketu."

This is quite a radical story. The universe, like the huge banyan tree, springs forth from the seed that contains nothing. Without a metaphor like the seed and the tree, our logical minds cannot even begin to imagine what such a large nothingness is since it is smaller than small and before the beginning.

The deeper mystery of this tale is that Svetaketu and his father were both made of the same all-pervading reality. In essence, they were from it.

'I am everything' implies an ability to transcend the normal flow of time and the normal confines of space. It makes everything possible. There are no limits except the ones we put on ourselves.

The ego finds the world a dangerous, hostile place because everything that exists is separate from 'I'. This is the condition known as duality and it is a great source of fear. In fact, the ancient Vedas called it the only source of fear.

Duality does exist and, because of its existence, the recognition of a higher unity is made meaningful. Two opposite poles fuse into a whole. This principle puts the silent and invisible and the active and visible aspects of life into proper perspective. When the ancient seers found union, they found the other aspect that makes life complete.

The same ancient text explains this ever-present reality as *purnam adah, puram idam*, implying 'This is full, that is full. From the full arises the full. If you take something away from that full, the full remains full.'

The highest goal of existence is to achieve 200 per cent of life. You can accomplish this because a human being is flexible enough to appreciate both the diversity of life, which is infinite but full of boundaries, and the state of union, which is equally infinite but completely unbound. No one was given a cosmic blueprint and instructed: Remember you can implement only half of it.

No one gave us any limitation on the patterns of thought we can have, change, blend, expand or create. Life is a field of unlimited possibilities. We must simply have the courage to become. In other words, the message of divinity seems to be:

Live life Godsize!

The pursuit of a treasured dream can completely transform us and the greatest gift we receive is the inner transformation that occurs.

The practice of Zen, with its illuminating wisdom, portrays courage as a tiny frail flower, growing among rocks, that has striven to reach the sun. Despite its vulnerability, it has had the courage to try. If it had been content to stay as a seed, its shell would have kept it safe for decades. But by keeping the world out, it would have also kept itself in. By striving to fulfil its destiny, it risked the dangers and pushed out into the unknown.

In Zen, the image of the flower battling to push past the rocks and soil and having the blind faith that there will be enough water and light to ensure its survival is a powerful representation of the trials we will also have to overcome in order to break through the shell of our old self and the limits of our old beliefs to discover who we really are and what we are actually capable of. We are like the flower, facing the same fears and unknown dangers of this world, armed only with our courage, our faith and the vision of what we intend to be.

A life without risk is a dangerous illusion. Run from life and it tends to chase you. Hide from it and it comes looking. But look your fears in the eye and they tend to blink first. This is the way to the evolution of the soul. What we call a safe life is not safe. There is no security. Ultimately the only thing you can have faith in is yourself. You are the only constant reality in your life. And wherever you go, there you are.

Many people in life fail to realise that their external reality is simply a reflection of their internal one. And so they look to other people and their environment to prop themselves up in the mistaken belief that they can be protected in life, wrapped up comfortably in a warm blanket. Careers and status may rise and fall, friends and family will pass away and lovers will come and go. All you have is who you are. All you have is your character. And even the fickle twist and turns of fate and life lose their terror when you cultivate the deep inner conviction that no matter what happens to you in life, you will be able to handle it. You will always be there for your own self.

The life you long to create and lead will only be achieved by drawing on the heroic aspect of yourself—your courage, your compassion, your daring and your determination. And most of all, your self-belief.

All is possible if you believe it.

Our lives are a function of our actions, and our actions are a function of our character. Our character arises from our courage. Never fear failure. Never fear of making mistakes. Fear only one thing—doing nothing. Banish pettiness, criticism, apathy and all the excuses of the timid mind from yourself and commit right now to living to the highest aspiration of your heart. Commit to living your life and be determined to live it…heroically.

As the age-old words of the enlightened Buddha remind us:

We are what we think;
all that we are arises with our thoughts.
With our thoughts
we make the world.

Often, I try to completely revolutionise my perspective by thinking of how God feels when He sees the way we are living our lives. What would He have us improve? What advice would He give us? Here is what I think He would say. I call it…

Memo from God

I see you, my children.
I see you, my children, and I am not happy.

Year after year, you run after your desires and chase empty,
unwholesome dreams, and when the resultant actions are upon you,
you twist the blame and complain to me.
I see you give away your birthright, your inherited gifts and
strengths, even convince yourself that you are weak and
incapable of true success and grandeur.
I see all this as I watch you play and I am not happy, not happy at all.

What happened to the two greatest gifts I gave you—your choice
and your will? What happened to the innate strength I pumped into
you even before you went to play your game, the innate strength
that only requires a spark of self-belief to surpass the bounds of all
other forms of energy now known to you?
What happened to the lessons of power with humility, softness with
resolve and, above all, the amazing power of prayer and surrender that you
learnt so well before you left home?

What have you done with all my great gifts?
How have you become so impotent that you conveniently blame
your circumstances for your own failures and mistakes?
How have you accepted the false belief that the only way to rise is
by pulling another down?
How have you given up belief in yourself to carry a belief
only in me?

Have I not told you repeatedly that you are my own, that all is possible for you, that you are in charge of your own game? That if you give up responsibility, I can never accept it, that I only help those who help themselves, that I am behind you to support you, but that you must walk on your own and that you and I together are always in the majority. That if you perform the right action, I shall send you the right fruit.

Why have you forgotten?
That you are the creator of your own destiny, that you are
in control as much as I am, that your pains and pleasures
are of your own making, that you are capable of miracles because
I stand behind your every step, that if you only seek my help
I shall fulfil you, that I am your only true friend, your only unchanging
lover, your only real guide.

No, I am not happy at all when I see you, my children.
It pains me to see what you have become,
how low you have stooped.
I made you strong and you have become weak.
I made you kings and you have become slaves.
I made you creators, and you have become merely the creation.

APPENDIX ONE

HOW TO BE EMPTY

We all need emptiness in our lives in order to learn more and to keep evolving. Most of us are full of ourselves. 'I', 'me' and 'mine' are usually the only motivations in our lives. We must, however, attempt to be empty in order to receive. For new things can come only when there is space for them. Here is a simple exercise that will help.

Sit in a quiet place where you will not be disturbed. Close your eyes and shed all thoughts about your life, family, relationships, career, wealth and so on. Accept that the entire universe is yours. And that this universe is a positive one. Acceptance of this thought will bring you peace of mind.

Realise that the outer world does not have to change first in order for your inner world to change. Be aware that the inner world changes the outer world faster than the other way around. So what you really need is a change in your beliefs. Emptiness and space is needed within you for this to happen.

Breathe deeply from your stomach. Do not hold your breath. Feel your mind emptying itself of all externals. Negative thoughts will begin to disappear and you will feel you are enveloped by positive energy coming to you from the universe. Now that your mind is empty, visualise what you want most in life, without putting any limits upon yourself. Build a castle in the air and then build a ladder to reach it. Let your imagination run wild. If it is wealth you are seeking, dream of it and how you will create it. After all, success is a state of mind and small successes will invariably lead to larger ones.

APPENDIX TWO

IS TRUE SUCCESS FOR YOU?

Answer 'Yes' or 'No'. Give yourself 1 point for a 'Yes' answer and 0 points for a 'No' answer.

1. Do you believe that you deserve to succeed?
2. Do you believe in action?
3. Are you willing to give what it takes?
4. Do you see the positive side in most things?
5. Can you fail and still learn?
6. Do you talk to people often with the idea of learning?
7. Are you aware of your habits, both good and bad?
8. Are you open to growth and change?
9. Do you believe you are friendly?
10. Can you remember the lessons you learnt from your mistakes?
11. Can you list down your mistakes?
12. Can you remain calm despite being surrounded by disruptive people in disturbing circumstances?

What your score says:

Below 5: Forget success, change yourself first

5 to 8: Work on yourself, success awaits you

Above 8: Success calls you, do not delay

APPENDIX THREE

TOOLS FOR SELF-TRANSFORMATION

The three powerful techniques discussed below have been developed from a system called psychosynthesis that was created by Italian psychiatrist Roberto Assagioli. This system has paved the way for the use of creative visualisation and imagery to facilitate personal growth.

THE DIAMOND

Diamond is created by the immense heat and pressure that it has endured over thousands of years. Its trials create its beauty. The word 'diamond' comes from the Greek word *adamas*, which means 'unconquerable'.

Visualise a diamond in your mind's eye. See its perfection, its beauty. It has many sides, many facets, but it is one whole. As you quietly meditate upon this diamond, understand that you are not your fears or worries. You are not your job or your habits. Your self is as perfect as the diamond. It is unconquerable, eternal. Let this image and its meaning flow through you. Then, when you are ready, take the image of the diamond and place it within your heart.

This very simple visualisation instills in us serenity and a deep inner confidence that no matter how bad things get, our true identity, our self, remains unconquerable. We may be experiencing bad times but they are only experiences. Our true self cannot be harmed.

THE CORK

The image of the cork is a powerful communicator of our ability to stay afloat no matter what life throws at us or how stormy it gets.

Close your eyes and imagine you are a cork bobbing about in the middle of the sea. The sea is calm, the sun is shining and the sky is clear. Now imagine clouds gathering and the sea becoming choppy. The skies darken and thunder roars as a storm breaks. You are being tossed about in the waves, battered from side to side. Huge waves crash down, covering you. Make the storm as bad and the seas as rough as you can. Really experience the feelings of a horrific sea storm. But no matter how bad it gets, you keep bobbing back to the surface. You cannot sink, no matter how perilous the conditions, because it is in your nature to float.

After a while, imagine the sea calming down and the sun coming out. The sun warms your face and there you are, a little cork bobbing away on the surface, unsinkable, able to weather any storm.

Those of us who are blessed with optimism or prone to despair simply use imaginary and internal metaphors that either support or depress us. By using our imagination, we take control of processes that were previously occurring beneath the surface of our souls.

THE LIGHTHOUSE

Imagine yourself on a small ship in the middle of the ocean. It is pitch-black, a storm is raging and the ship is rolling from side to side. You are desperately trying to steer as the rain batters down on your face and the wind howls around you. Experience this as vividly as you can. Feel the fatigue in your muscles and your fear increase as the realisation sets in that you are totally lost and will soon succumb to the storm.

Suddenly, in the distance, you see a brilliant light piercing the darkness. The light is coming from a lighthouse. You know now that all you have to do is follow its unwavering light and you will be safe. Feel the sense of security and relief that comes with seeing the lighthouse. As you draw near, you can see the magnificence of its structure as it stands above the waves, solid upon the rocks. Now as you look up at it, feel your unwavering strength and security. You are your own security, your own guide. You light the path to your future and are the rock upon which it will be built.

You are all that you need.

Do not underestimate the power of harnessing our imagination. Albert Einstein developed the theory of relativity by imagining he was riding on a beam of light into space. Many psychiatrists have proven that in contests between willpower and imagination, our imagination always wins.

APPENDIX FOUR

25 QUALITIES OF A SUCCESSFUL PERSON

Here is a list of 25 qualities that almost all self-created leaders and the wealthy people of this world share. Try and imbibe them into your life.

1. Have a strong self-belief
2. Take responsibility for your actions and life
3. Believe in action as well as in prayer
4. Be self-aware
5. Don't major in minor things
6. Be disciplined
7. Be an avid reader
8. Be a copious notetaker
9. Understand the value of enthusiasm
10. Be adaptable and able to improvise
11. Be optimistic
12. Be a good time manager
13. Be a good listener
14. Be a good communicator
15. Do not be afraid to take calculated risks
16. Learn from mistakes
17. Be able to adjust action to reality

18. Be persistent and persevering
19. Have the ability to identify and use moods
20. Be able to step out of the comfort zone
21. Be a visionary with patience
22. Enjoy work
23. Be focused
24. Be a quick decision-maker
25. Be able to handle criticism, rejection and frustration

SUGGESTED READING

The Art of Worldly Wisdom. Baltasar Gracián (trans. by Joseph Jacobs) (Shambhala Publications, 1993)

As a Man Thinketh. James Allen (Mindart Publishing Co., 1988)

The Bhagvadgita. Narahari D. Parikh (ed.) (Greenleaf Books, 1984)

Creators on Creating: Awakening and Cultivating the Imaginative Mind. Frank Barron, Alfonso Montuori, Anthea Barron (eds.) (J.P. Tarcher, 1997)

Dhammapada: Wisdom of the Buddha. Hariscandra Kavirakna (ed.) (Theosophical University Press, 1980)

The Energy of Money: A Spiritual Guide to Financial and Personal Fulfillment. Maria Nemeth (Wellspring/Ballantine, 1999)

How to Make Money out of Thin Air. Brian Sher (Penguin, 2002)

How to Think Like a Millionaire. Charles Albert Poissant (HarperCollins, 1989)

The Law of Success: The 21st-Century Edition. Napoleon Hill (High Roads Media, 2004)

Manifest Your Destiny: The Nine Spiritual Principles for Getting Everything You Want. Wayne W. Dyer (HarperTorch, 1999)

The One Minute Millionaire: The Enlightened Way to Wealth. Mark Victor Hansen and Robert G. Allen (Harmony Books, 2002)

Real Success: Based on the Writings of Success *Magazine Founder Orison Swett Marden*. Ken Shelton and the editors of *Success* Magazine (Executive Excellence, 1999)

The Tao of Abundance. Laurence G. Boldt. (Penguin, 1999)

"The Yoga of Wealth takes participants through a mind-shattering journey..."
The Eternal Solutions magazine, India

"Malkani puts forward the fact that success is not only the fruit, but also the root and the entire journey. One still works hard but the struggle seems to cease."
Training and Management magazine, India

"Vikas Malkani teaches people to 'live life Godsize'."
The Pioneer, India

"The guru of the rich and famous now teaches you their secrets."
Guts and Glory, India

"The jeans guru who gave up a business empire."
The New Paper, Singapore

"I found Vikas's way of communicating knowledge delightfully simple, clear and thorough. And he answered all my questions."
Ming Chien, Technopreneur

"Vikas has a gift for simplifying what is profound, sometimes by using stories, which makes his messages powerful and memorable. For me, the most important insight was that success happens inside-out, and that the circle begins with me. I learnt to use my strengths to take me where I want to go, to discover what I am passionate about and, above all, to 'live life Godsize'. It was a wonderful experience full of learning and love. I highly recommend it."

Sally Forrest Sargison

"With Yoga of Wealth, Vikas has created the ideal balance between spirituality and wealth, the inner and outer worlds and our desires and their realisation. Vikas is one of the most wonderful teachers of transformational wisdom I have experienced."

Eugenia Gajardo, meditation teacher and founder of KnowThySelf